NEW YORK

A PICTURE MEMORY

Text
Bill Harris

Captions
Pauline Graham

Design
Teddy Hartshorn

Photography
Colour Library Books Ltd
FPG International
George Freston
International Stock Photo
The Telegraph Colour Library

Picture Research
Annette Lerner

Commissioning Editor
Andrew Preston

Editorial
Gill Waugh

Production
Ruth Arthur
David Proffit
Sally Connolly

Director of Production
Gerald Hughes

Director of Publishing
David Gibbon

CLB 2504
© 1990 Colour Library Books Ltd, Godalming, Surrey, England.
All rights reserved.
Color separations by Scantrans Pte Ltd, Singapore.
This 1990 edition published by Crescent Books,
distributed by Outlet Book Company, Inc, a Random House Company,
225 Park Avenue South, New York, New York 10003.
Printed and bound in Italy.
ISBN 0 517 01740 7
8 7 6 5 4 3 2 1

NEW YORK
A PICTURE MEMORY

CRESCENT BOOKS
NEW YORK

Back in 1932, a New Yorker who took a back seat to no one in his love of what they called the Empire City in those days, predicted what life might be like fifty years in the future, in 1982. He said that if population growth continued over the following 50 years at the same rate it had over the previous half-century, there would be 50 million New Yorkers by 1982. His guess was that New York's population was about seven million at the time, and it was already a crowded place. But he predicted that the overflow would make it necessary for the city to absorb "a goodly share of Long Island," plus Yonkers, White Plains and most of the territory north of the city. He said that the East River would have been filled in by then, and thousands of acres of the Hudson River reclaimed.

The city's population did grow over those 50 years, but not by much. The 1986 census counted only 7,262,700. He had based his prediction on the incredible growth of the second half of the 19th century, when the number almost quintupled. But even what the Census Bureau calls the New York Consolidated Metropolitan Statistical Area, which extends into New Jersey and Connecticut and includes the still unannexed territory on Long Island as well as the cities and towns to the north, reported just under 18 million in 1986. It's a long way from 50 million, but it's still five million more than the Los Angeles CMSA, and ten million more than Chicago and its suburbs.

There are nearly 1.5 million people crammed into Manhattan's 22.6 square miles, more than in all 136 square miles of Philadelphia. If it were a city all by itself, which it was until 1898, it would edge out Philadelphia as America's fifth-largest. The Borough of Brooklyn as an independent city would rank fourth, ahead of Houston, Texas, by more than a half-million. And the number swells every weekday when more people than live in Minneapolis travel into Manhattan by train, bus and private car, some of them spending as many as two hours getting to work, not because getting there is half the fun, but because being there is all there is for people who sincerely want to get rich. The man who looked into New York's future back in 1932 saw that coming.

"Those who for some reason still prefer to sleep in Chicago," he said, "may be included among New York's commuters." In a way he was right. The three airports that serve New York handle more than 75 million passengers a year, and a good percentage are business travelers. And if they're not commuters in the same sense as the people on the 7:56 from Babylon, they make it their business to get to New York as often as they can.

His prediction that the East River would have vanished by now, leaving South Street Seaport landlocked, and depriving us of the view of the Brooklyn Bridge from Pier Seventeen, didn't work out. The East River is still handling the tides between Long Island Sound and the Atlantic Ocean, and though a good deal of landfill has been added to the Hudson, giving us, among other things, all of the World Financial Center, there doesn't seem to be much danger that the river will ever stop flowing down from the Adirondacks past the the Statue of Liberty and out to sea.

He said that by the 1980s buildings would be at least 250 stories high and that the elevators in them would be triple-decked affairs that would whisk tenants upward at speeds "surpassing all imagination at this time." He had seen double-deck elevators in the 1932 Cities Service Building on Pine Street, but it wasn't until 1978, when Citicorp built its slant-roofed tower on Lexington Avenue and made its elevators double-deckers, that anyone imitated them and there still doesn't seem to be any future for elevators that serve more than one floor at a time. The best New York could do to fulfill his dream of higher skyscrapers is the World Trade Center's twin towers which, at 110 stories each, were the tallest buildings in the world for a couple of weeks back in 1973 before an upstart in Chicago known as the Sears Tower took the title away. The World Trade Center's 104 elevators whisk passengers the 1350 feet to the top so fast your ears hardly have time to pop, but not really fast enough to beggar the imagination or to leave your stomach behind.

He was convinced that well before the last quarter of the twentieth century, elevated railroads would be multi-tiered and the trains noiseless. They were both reasonable assumptions. The elevated system had seventeen double-deck stations at the time, and noisy, steam-powered trains had been replaced by quieter and cleaner electric power back in 1903. But he was wrong again on both counts. The last of Manhattan's elevated railroads vanished from Third Avenue in 1956, three years after the fare on the entire transit system was raised to fifteen cents and subway tokens were introduced for the first time. The trains that rush over the 708 miles of track in the subway system today are quieter than they were in 1932, but it's still hard to hear yourself think on a busy platform when the uptown and downtown expresses roar in at the same time. He didn't make any predictions about what it would cost to take a ride on one of those trains in the 1980s. But it should be noted that it cost a nickel in his day, and nobody's making any predictions about how high the fare can go.

Back in the early 1930s everyone seriously believed that it would be just a matter of time before fast food would be the only kind available. But they weren't thinking about fake hamburgers. They were looking forward to the day when a seven-course dinner would be reduced to a capsule that could be swallowed on the run, and in that vein, our seer looked into his crystal ball and saw that well before the 1980s, "restaurants, cafes and dining places generally will probably be passé." Fortunately, he was wrong again. At last count, there were 25,000 restaurants in the city. If the entire population of Pottstown, Pennsylvania, arrived in New York at the same time, they could each have dinner in a different restaurant, and what an adventure it would be. Some could sample the fare of Thailand, others of the Ukraine; they could try saag gosht at an Indian table or start a meal with some spicy mezedakia at a Greek taverna. Some of them might look for a "New York-cut" steak, which appears on menus in every city in the United States, except New York. In the Big Apple, they call it sirloin, and order it "blood rare."

New Yorkers are almost obsessed by food, and it's a rare conversation among them that doesn't touch on some new restaurant or an old favorite rediscovered. But that's not the reason why they proudly call their city "the Big Apple." It's a term that existed back in the early 1930s, but only among jazz musicians who had taken the name of a popular dance craze and made it a code word for New York. Back then, most of them earned their living playing one-night stands in college towns and small cities across the country. They spent their days sleeping in a bus on the way to the next gig and dreaming of moving to New York. It represented the Big Time and it was every bit as tempting to them as Eve's forbidden fruit. And, best of all, at the end of a night's work in a hotel ballroom, a nightclub or in the orchestra pit of a Broadway theater, a guy could go home and sleep in a real bed. The name stayed in the underground until the 1970s, when the New York Convention and Visitors Bureau brought it out, dusted it off and made it the core of their advertising campaign.

Summing up New York into a single image is a formidable challenge, and when the apple began appearing on posters and in shop windows, no one would have predicted that it would still be there nearly twenty years later. But except for cab drivers who say it's going downhill and Wall Street types who bet on the future every day, New Yorkers stopped making predictions about their city more than a generation ago. About the only safe forecast is that New York will be different tomorrow than it is today. And that's one of the things that makes it exciting. In spite of a Landmarks Commission dedicated to preserving old neighborhoods, Old New York doesn't really exist. There are a few structures like Gracie Mansion, where the Mayor lives, that date back to colonial times, but none to remind us that this was once a Dutch town complete with canals, windmills and step-gabled roofs.

But today's New Yorkers pay homage to the Dutch Founding Fathers every business day. The Dutch West India Company established Nieuw Amsterdam with no other purpose than to make money, and they would put up with almost anything from the settlers as long as their profit margins were good. When the British took over in 1664 and called it New York, the Dutch businessmen kept right on making money as though nothing had happened. And when New York became the first capital of the United States, Alexander Hamilton compromised with the other politicians to allow them to relocate a bit further south as long as New York stayed the country's financial capital.

It still is. Seven of the ten biggest banks in the United States are in New York, as well as four of the six largest insurance companies. And with two stock exchanges, it's the place the whole world looks to for the answer to the age-old question, "how's business?" But there's more to New York business than moving dollars around. Its harbor, the country's biggest, handles more than two million tons of cargo a year. The fashion industry keeps more than 5,000 New York companies humming and adds some $14 billion to the city's economy each year. And if there's no business like show business, consider that more than eight million people see a Broadway show in an average year, not even counting Off Broadway and Off-Off Broadway; and that of the 350 films released by Hollywood in 1988, 115 were shot either completely or in part "on location" in New York. Add the production of television shows and commercials and it comes to $2.3 billion a year.

But if all those numbers suggest that New York is a corporate town, there are more than 360,000 people who have shunned the rat race and gone into business for themselves. Not all of them will still be in business at the end of the year, but each and every year some 5,000 new entrepreneurs join the ranks of the self-employed.

And every year, New York is invaded by thousands who know it is only a matter of time before they set the town on its ear. Their average age is 22 to 29. They're college-educated. And they're eager, even excited. Over the last two decades, they have represented the fastest-growing segment of New York's population, giving the city America's biggest net increase in that age group.

Traditionally, young people migrating to New York have been aspiring actors and artists, musicians and writers. And they are still arriving every day of the week. But in the last few years, more and more people in their twenties have been moving to New York in search of a business career. Some of them are new lawyers, others have fresh MBA diplomas tucked into their briefcases. Often as not, they'll say that New York is just a way station for them. They know they'll find more job opportunities in New York, but more important they'll get on the job training that will make them more valuable to an employer when they go home again, which they'll tell you in all seriousness is exactly what they're planning to do. But once they get to New York, something mysterious happens. They themselves provide a spark to the New York atmosphere that no other city can match. Then the spark turns to fire, and before you know it, they're hooked. Peoria never looks quite the same again.

Obviously, one of the things that makes New York attractive to them is all the other people in the same age group who they can meet and share their dreams with. An artist who came to experiment, an actress who works part-time as a waitress to give her more time to go to auditions and classes, a music student who makes ends meet by giving impromptu recitals on a Fifth Avenue street corner, all have one very important thing in common: each other. They find the diversity exhilarating, too. They give New York a huge measure of its vitality and excitement, and that's precisely what they came here to find in the first place. In the end, it's what keeps them here, too.

Newcomers usually arrive with some trepidation after hearing wild and woolly stories usually ending with the observation that if New York is a nice place to visit, it's also a terrible place to live. No one who lives in New York would say that, and new arrivals soon find themselves wondering how such a myth got started in the first place. Out-of-towners will say that "people can live in one of those big apartment houses for years and never get to know their next-door neighbor. You could die there and nobody would know, much less care." The fact is, most New Yorkers do know their neighbors, and many of them know as much about each other as people in small towns where everybody is probably related to each other. The difference is that where space is limited, people have a tendency to respect each other's share of it. New Yorkers are very good at that, but they do sincerely care about each other.

The city is broken down into convenient neighborhoods, and anyone who has lived in one of them for more than a few weeks is probably on a first-name basis with the dry cleaner, the newsstand operator, the super market check-out clerk. They feel genuine sympathy for the shoe repair man whose landlord has just raised his rent by $2500 a month. They have their favorite neighborhood restaurant where they know they'll meet good friends on evenings when cooking at home doesn't seem like the perfect way to end a busy day. When they're out jogging or walking the dog it's inevitable that they'll stop to chat a minute of two with somebody from the neighborhood about what's going to happen to that expensive storefront now that the shoemaker has been forced to move out, and the conversation will probably lead to where to take their running shoes for repairs now that he's gone.

Visitors get a taste of their friendliness and pride simply by standing on midtown street corners with a look of confusion and an unfolded map. Sometimes the advice they get is wrong, but the spirit is there. Even some natives don't know that the number four bus on Madison Avenue will get you all the way up to the Cloisters at both the other end and the other side of the island. Yes, there are some things New Yorkers don't know. But you'll never catch one admitting it.

Public transportation can get you anywhere you need to go. It's why most Manhattanites don't own their own cars. That same bus that takes you up to the Cloisters runs downtown to Madison Square Garden, which may seem a strange cultural juxtaposition until you realize that New York City is full of them. But the best way to capture the essence of the place is on foot. There are some people who live in New York who still don't know that, but during a transit strike a few years ago thousands found out and since then the best way to spot a real New Yorker is to look for someone smartly dressed but wearing sneakers. Young women executives with trim skirts and blazers and glasses casually perched on top of their heads have started carrying tote bags along with their soft briefcases to accommodate the high-heeled shoes they'll wear in the office.

What makes walking such an adventure is the incredible variety of faces and street theater you see at every turn along the way. On the upper East Side, the people who run the designer boutiques along Madison Avenue thoughtfully change their window displays every week. If your route takes you through the Garment Center along Seventh Avenue below 42d Street, you'll find many of the 300,000 people who work there at work on the streets, pushing bolts of cloth on hand trucks or finished dresses on racks. You'll see salesmen pushing waist-high sample cases and knots of people standing in the middle of the sidewalk engrossed in the New York outdoor sport called "schmoosing." On the West Side, the people will be casually dressed in studied costumes they hope will make them look "creative." On the East Side, your fellow-walkers will be more stylishly dressed in outfits they hope will make them look successful.

But wherever you go in New York, the people are all interesting, if not beautiful. There's a vitality there that is infectious. Even if they are not "making it," it's a rare New Yorker who doesn't expect to any day now. And they'll all be pleased to tell you that making it in New York is a tough proposition. They're probably right. But at this moment there are more than seven million people accepting the challenge and most of them wouldn't trade places with anyone.

Liberty Enlightening the World, *better known as the Statue of Liberty (facing page), was presented to the United States on July 4, 1886, by France at the suggestion of its Alsatian sculptor Frédéric Auguste Bartholdi. The figure was raised with the help of a supporting framework designed by Alexandre Gustave Eiffel.*

The Empire State Building (these pages), prodding the sky on 5th Avenue and 34th Street in midtown Manhattan (overleaf), is known by New York's nickname: "the Empire State." At 1,472 feet tall with 102 stories, it was the world's highest building from the time of its completion in May, 1931, until 1954. It now ranks third tallest next to, in ascending order, the World Trade Center, New York, and the Sears Roebuck Building, Chicago. The Empire State Building was completed in an amazing nineteen months – often with more than one whole story going up in a day. This world-famous landmark has been hung with many strange things, ranging from airships to a famous fictional giant gorilla called King Kong. One foggy morning in 1945 it even withstood a B-25 bomber crashing into it.

Facing page: almost symbolic gold is deflected from the glass of Manhattan's Financial District and slung out across the Hudson River. Sometimes the World Trade Center and its Plaza (below and below left) take on the color of a still more precious metal: platinum. Cesar Pelli's buildings, constituting the World Financial Center, stand before the twin towers of the World Trade Center and are topped with slow-weathering copper roofs. Left: the observatory deck of the World Trade Center, and (overleaf) an Uptown view of Manhattan, its nighttime streets looking like rivers of molten light.

South Street Seaport (these pages) is bounded by Fulton, Front, Beekman and Water streets. Fulton Landing (facing page) is named after Robert Fulton, who designed the first successful steamboat after giving up an unpromising career as an artist. The steamboat was not his only water-going invention. In 1797 he journeyed to Paris in order to sell the French his newly invented submarine, Nautilus, which could set powder charges under the hulls of British ships. At the time, the French government rejected the whole concept of submarine warfare as an atrocious and dishonorable way to fight, but by 1800 they had changed their tune and were ready to try out Nautilus. However, adverse weather conditions enabled the two target ships to outrun Fulton's slower creation. South Street Seaport is the last vestige of a nineteenth-century port in thriving Manhattan. Vintage sailing ships are docked here at restored piers, overlooked by the nineteenth-century, Federal-style brick houses of Schemerhorn Row.

Above: 5th Avenue, hung with flags. The cast-iron clock (below) on 5th Avenue at 44th Street dates from 1907 and was made by Seth Thomas for the American Trust Company. It stood outside their offices on 43rd Street for many years before being moved to its present site, and is a rare survivor from the turn of the century. Above left: the Grand Hyatt Hotel on Park Avenue, and (below left) the Helmsley Palace Hotel on Madison Avenue. Left and facing page: the Trump Tower, and (overleaf) Manhattan's sun-burnished Financial District.

Central Park (these pages and overleaf) was the idea of William Cullen Bryant, poet and editor, who suggested that a "pestilential spot where rank vegetation and miasmic odors taint every breath of air" be transformed into a public park. Above: Beresford Apartments, built by the self-taught architect Emery Roth on Central Park West, overlooking Bethesda Fountain. Facing page top: the slender, lantern-topped tower of the Sherry-Netherland Hotel and the splendid, copper-roofed Plaza Hotel, both overlooking the Pond.

41

Winter in New York City is cold. Daytime temperatures are often around thirty-two degrees Fahrenheit and rafts of ice float under Brooklyn Bridge (below), forming broken plates over the city's harbors (these pages). Left: the white United Nations' Building, and (facing page top) Battery Park. Battery Park City lies in front of the World Trade Center and was formed from material excavated during the World Trade Center's construction. Facing page bottom: New York Harbor at the mouth of the Hudson River, with South Street Seaport in the background.

In 1909, when its architect Henry Fornbostel first saw the completed Queensboro Bridge (below left) he said: "My God, it's a blacksmith shop!" In 1830 the elegant, arched granite towers of Brooklyn Bridge (below and bottom left) inspired Hart Crane to write: "How could mere toil align thy choiring strings!" Its choiring strings were tested for strength by P.T. Barnum, who paraded twelve elephants over it in 1884. Left: Manhattan Bridge.

Below and below left: the covered plaza of the I.B.M. Building on East 57th Street. The covered atrium (left) of the Citicorp Center in midtown Manhattan is a very pleasant spot to pause for coffee and a chat. Above left and above: 5th Avenue seen from the street and from the sky. Battery Park (facing page) is a wonderful vantage point from which to view Manhattan while walking along paths lined with tulips and cherry trees in bloom.

The Corinthian façade of the New York Stock Exchange (right) faces onto Broad Street, the figures on its carved pediment symbolizing commerce. The building is overlooked by the 1833 bronze statue of George Washington, erected outside Federal Hall. He took his presidential oath from the balcony of the original hall in 1789. The pedestal is said to contain a stone from the spot where he stood on that day. Below: the Stock Exchange trading floor, a riot of business. At the end of 5th Avenue, Washington Square Park is announced by Stanford White's Washington Arch (facing page), now almost a symbol of Greenwich Village.

Doyers Street (left) in the city's Chinatown exemplifies the color and variety of Manhattan streets. Red, the prevalent color of Chinatown's signs, combines vibrancy with good fortune: for the Chinese, red is the color of good luck. To sustain the crowds thronging Manhattan's streets, street vendors sell cool drinks (below) and fresh pretzels (above). On Sundays Orchard Street (above left, below left and facing page) on the Lower East Side is closed to traffic and pedestrians are able to throng to the shops.

The Statue of Liberty (below), apparently modeled on the artist's mother, by all accounts a formidable woman, watches over Manhattan's Financial District (these pages) from Upper New York Bay. The golden pyramid of the 1928 New York Life Insurance Company Building (overleaf) on Madison Avenue stands over the site of Stanford White's old Madison Square Gardens. In 1906, White was shot on the roof of the old building by Harry K. Thaw, husband of Evelyn Nesbitt, White's former mistress.

Left: New York Rangers ice hockey team in Madison Square Gardens. Above left and below left: Manhattan's Museum of Modern Art, and (below) the Metropolitan Museum of Art. Above: Jean Dubuffet's Group of Four Trees in Chase Manhattan Plaza – not a sculpture, but "an unleashed graphism." Facing page: (bottom) Frank Lloyd Wright's Guggenheim Museum, and (top) the Metropolitan Opera House, in the Lincoln Center, spilling out its beautifully dressed clientèle.

A fork of light (facing page) is created in Manhattan's nightscape (these pages, overleaf and following page) by the Flatiron Building, which rises like the prow of a ship at the head of Ladies' Mile. At 300 feet tall, the Flatiron, or Fuller Building, as it was originally called, was the world's tallest building when it was completed in 1902. Lights hang on Manhattan like evening accessories, outlining Pier 17 (overleaf) of South Street Seaport (below) and giving Liberty (right) a twinkling solitaire.

61

Homestyle

THAI AND INDONESIAN

Cooking

by
SRI OWEN

THE CROSSING PRESS
FREEDOM, CALIFORNIA

Published in the U.S.A. in 1997 by The Crossing Press.
© 1988 Sri Owen
Published in the U.K. in 1988 by
Judy Piatkus (Publishers) Limited

Cover design by Victoria May
Design by Paul Saunders
Boxed illustrations by Soun Vannithone
Food for photography cooked by Sri Owen
Photography by Tim Intrie
This book was set in New Baskerville

For information on bulk purchases or group discounts for this and other Crossing Press titles,
please contact our Special Sales Manager at 800-777-1048.

Visit our Web site on the Internet at:
www.crossingpress.com

ISBN 0-89594-859-1

ACKNOWLEDGMENTS

Many people have helped, directly and indirectly, in the research and preparation of this book. In particular, there are many friends in Jakarta, Yogyakarta, and elsewhere—we were all students together, once upon a time—they are too many for me to name, but I am grateful to all of them. I would particularly like to mention the following, as long as it is understood that they are not responsible for whatever errors have made their way into my text. First, my five sisters: Sumarni Syamsi in Magelang, Central Java; Harmini Djamil in Bandung; Ratnasari and her husband Haikal Salam in Pontianak, West Kalimantan; Roslina Usman in Jakarta; and Nurmalina Anwar, also in Pontianak. My brother-in-law, Usman Beka, helped me greatly by introducing me to people and making my travel arrangements, while Nurdiana Basuki patiently found books for me and answered innumerable questions. Among many friends in Yogyakarta, I must record the names of Soeatminah and of Ahmad Wirono

and his wife. In Bali, Anak Agung Gde Rai and his wife, and Suryasih Mudita were especially helpful and hospitable.

In Bangkok, I received help, generosity, and encouragement from two old friends, formerly of the Thai Section at the BBC, Kamolvan Punyashthiti and Sombat Bhuapirom, and from Mrs. Punyashthiti's mother, Kunying Thavil Prakop Nitisar. They took enormous trouble to make sure that I saw and tasted everything, and they introduced me to dishes, recipes, restaurants, and chefs that were vital to my purpose in writing the book.

In London, I thank my two editors, Gill Cormode and Veronica Sperling, who have put a lot of their own enthusiasm into the book as well as their professional expertise. Another old friend who has contributed a great deal to my knowledge of Indonesian cooking is Fatimah Yahya. Several of these recipes came originally from her.

TO ROGER

CONTENTS

FOREWORD

A new book by Sri Owen is a happy event, and I embrace the opportunity to celebrate it. It is not just that she is a marvelously good cook and a fine writer, nor just that her amiable personality suffuses what she writes with a special charm. There is a further cause for celebration. The cuisines of which she writes, unlike those of most European countries and North America, have not been the subject of numerous books. Much remains to be told.

Living and traveling in Southeast Asia in the mid-1970s, I quickly realized how good the food was, and how varied from country to country and region to region. I also discovered the paucity of good written material about it. In many European countries there is a long line of cookbooks stretching back to the Middle Ages. Not so in Southeast Asia.

This contrast does not reflect a lack of material. A dispassionate comparison of the cuisine of, say, Spain with that of Thailand, or the Netherlands with Indonesia, or England with Malaysia, is enough to show that. Yet, because of the lack of books, the cuisines of Southeast Asia have until recently attracted less attention than they deserve.

Anyone dealing with a part of Southeast Asia is bound to be tempted to cross national boundaries and explore neighboring parts. The countries are like a string of jewels, or rather strings, for one can link them in various ways. One string starts in the Asian subcontinent and goes from Burma to Thailand and on to Malaysia and Indonesia and the Philippines. As in the game of "Gossip," the starting point and the end are dissimilar, but at each step there are clear similarities to be observed. The web of influences and connections would take a lifetime to disentangle, especially if the pervasive influence of China and the Chinese overseas communities were taken into account, plus culinary currents flowing from the Indian subcontinent and weird relics from colonial regimes. Most people would rather just enjoy the dishes than probe into their history. All the same, it is very interesting to have two of the cuisines juxtaposed, as in this book, and to sense something of their relationship.

In a recent essay, M. F. K. Fisher sounded a warning, disconcerting note about people "who love to cook." Under her remorseless analysis, the statement "I love to cook" is perceived to have hidden meanings such as "I love power, and control of the kitchen gives it to me." No doubt M. F. K. Fisher is right, in a general way, but I wish that she could meet Sri Owen, for I am sure that she would at once admit that here is an exception, a cook who in a completely uncomplicated way really does just love to cook—and to share her knowledge and enthusiasm with all of us.

Alan Davidson

INTRODUCTION

This book is full of recipes, but it is really about food. I have no special wish to start people making monster *rijsttafels* or hunting exotic spices for authentic ethnic meals. The recipes are authentic, of course, but the ingredients should be quite easy to find in most large cities. By all means cook complete Indonesian or Thai meals—you can scarcely go wrong! But my real purpose is to introduce ingredients, flavors, techniques. Those who cook their way through this book will, I think, develop a real insight into the way we cook and eat in Indonesia and Thailand today— not so much in the villages, where tradition is still strong, but in the big cities where all sorts of interesting changes are happening: folkways developing into lifestyles, new cuisines growing out of the old.

For example, it used to be the custom to put all the food on the table at once and let everyone help themselves. The "help yourself" rule still applies, but the average family meal is now often served in a sequence of courses, and the total number of dishes is smaller than it used to be because when the housewife (or the husband) cooks there is not enough time to make anything too elaborate.

Any of the dishes in this book will fit very happily into a diverse menu that may otherwise be European, Chinese, Mexican, or what you will. I have cooked all the dishes in this book, and if you follow the recipes exactly you will get excellent results—but once you are familiar with the things we do to food, feel free to adapt and improvise, inventing your own variations on Thai curries and

Market stall in Yogyakarta

Indonesian *sambal goreng*. What matters is knowing what's good.

Thai and Indonesian food have much in common, and it makes sense to put them together in one book. There would be no excuse, though, for blurring the differences. Some ingredients are available in one country and not in the other; for example, there are no *kemiri*, or candlenuts, in Thailand. There are differences in taste: Indonesians dislike coriander root and leaves (known in other countries as cilantro), using only the seeds. Religion and custom play important roles in eating habits. Most Thais are Buddhists and those who are not vegetarians are willing to eat pork. Most Indonesians are Moslems and avoid pork. They eat lamb or goat, while the Thais do not eat lamb at all, except in the region close to the Malaysian border. These differences are real though both nations have very similar climates, soil, and produce.

I did all the research for this book in big cities—Bandung, Jakarta, Bangkok—and large provincial capitals: Yogyakarta in Central Java, and Pontianak in West Kalimantan. I have read somewhere that these cities are among the fastest-growing in the world, and I can believe it. The pace and the pressures are ruthless, exciting, frightening. Yogyakarta still has something of the atmosphere of cultured politeness that I remember from my student days there. Pontianak was a fishing village for centuries and later the seat of a minor Sultan. Now, with its broad river bringing logs by barges from the interior, and the fine new bridge taking the coast road across that river, it seems set to become the sago and plywood capital of the world.

In two words: traditions change. Wherever I went, I enjoyed lavish hospitality, as has always been our custom. I met friends and friends' friends and was asked into their houses and their kitchens, and I met restaurant owners, hotel managers, journalists, editors, and publishers. From what they told me and

showed me, I began to get some notion of the changes that are taking place, and of the underlying attitudes that are unchanged.

People's expectations are much higher than they once were. Thirty years ago, if your house had electricity at all, you thought yourself lucky to have forty watts—enough for one small light bulb. Today my sisters and their friends take it for granted that they will be able to run a refrigerator and a food processor, as well as have ample lighting and the inevitable color TV and video tape recorder. Electric ovens are also becoming fairly common, though freezers are still rare, perhaps because of operating costs.

In the shops you can buy imported foods—things like cheese and apples—which are by no means cheap but which in the sixties were scarcely to be found at all. And the local produce is as fine as ever, especially (it seemed to me) the fruits—above all, the durian. Durian, even in season, has become horribly expensive, but who cares? With my sister and her husband, we drove out to Bogor and filled the back of the jeep with durian lashed together in fours, along with freshly cut Bogor pineapples that smell as sweet and innocent as the durian smells corrupt.

It is the "middle class"—still a small minority in the population but far more numerous and better off than I remember them—who are changing the society. Their attitude toward food, on the other hand, has not changed as much as it may appear.

The domestic traditions remain. Food is bought fresh whenever possible, though the daily visit to the market, which I used to enjoy so much in the cool of early morning, has been replaced by a weekly or biweekly trip to load up the car. Food is never wasted if it can possibly be saved and used. Domestic pets eat up the leftovers. My pampered London cat insists on meat; Indonesian cats seem to thrive on rice. Guests are welcomed at any time, invited or not; those who are invited may bring others with them, or may not turn up at all. Servants and hangers-on are fed; one lady I met in Bangkok provides lunch every working day for the staff of her son's garage business—180 of them.

The biggest change is that the housewife tends to leave much less to the cook than she used to, while her husband and children may well come into the kitchen to help or to take over. Cookbooks, virtually unknown not so long ago, are now best-sellers, and food-related journalism is becoming big business.

Cooking is really only a small part of the day's work. Wives in Thailand and Indonesia have careers; this is partly because they need the money but mostly because they have never submitted to being housebound by chores and children. Even one servant gives a wife a lot of freedom. But with only one servant, the family must do something for themselves, and cooking is most people's first choice. There's also the health angle, of course. The more diet-conscious people become, the stronger their desire to get into the kitchen.

So, inevitably, there arises a demand for convenience food, recipes that are quick and easy to make, ingredients that have been processed before they are bought. You can see the changes in the markets—not just the new supermarkets in the cities, which are becoming pretty much like the ones I am used to in London, but the much older street markets and those in smaller towns as well. Side by side with whole coconuts, coriander seeds, and chiles are grated fresh coconut flesh, ground coriander, and crushed chiles, prepackaged in little plastic bags. How hygienic the new ways are is debatable, but they are a boon to those without food processors. In Denpasar, the capital of Bali, you can buy spices in exactly the quantities you need for the dish you are going to cook, and you can ask the meat-seller in the market to cut the meat especially for you and even to advise you on how to cook it.

I have included notes on spices and sauces that may be unfamiliar to Western readers, but if some ingredients are not available to you, don't hesitate to substitute according to your imagination and experience. The result may not be strictly "authentic," but it will be well-cooked, interesting, and delicious.

SPECIALTY INGREDIENTS AND SUBSTITUTES

CANDLENUTS
(Aleurites moluccana)

Indonesian, *kemiri*. These are similar to macadamia nuts, but not quite the same. They are used in many Indonesian recipes, always crushed or ground before being mixed with other ingredients. You can use raw macadamia nuts as a satisfactory substitute. Don't eat candlenuts raw—they are mildly toxic until cooked.

CHILES
(Capsicum annuum, C. frutescens)

Indonesian, *cabé;* Thai, *prik.* Chiles are not native to Thailand or Indonesia. They were introduced to this area in the sixteenth century, when seeds and plants were brought from Central America. There are of course several kinds of chiles. The smallest chiles are the hottest, and the hottest part of the chiles is the seeds. That's why many of these recipes tell you to take the seeds out. Chiles can irritate the skin, especially if you are not accustomed to handling them. Rub a little salt on your hands before you start cutting them up, and wash your hands afterwards. Keep your hands away from your face and eyes while working with chiles. If you do get a little of the juice in

your eye, it will sting uncomfortably; wash the area with plenty of cold water.

CILANTRO
(Coriandrum sativum)

Indonesians use only coriander, the seeds of the cilantro plant. In Thailand they use the leaves as well as the seeds.

COCONUT, COCONUT MILK

Indonesian, *kelapa;* Thai, *maprao.* Coconuts play a central role in the cooking of Southeast Asia. Young coconuts are rarely available in Europe or North America. (I once had one in my shop—it was a lovely fresh green, but it must have been lying about its age because one morning it exploded and spattered everything and everybody with fermented coconut water.) The "fresh" brown hairy ones you buy in the supermarket are fine, and for a few of these recipes I think it is worth the trouble of cracking one open and prying out the flesh. This always comes away from the shell with a brown skin on its surface. If the flesh is to be used for making coconut milk, this brown skin need not be cut away because its color will not affect the finished dish. If, however, the flesh is to be used in a salad or a sweet, the

15

brown skin should be peeled off and discarded before grating the coconut.

Coconut milk

(*santen* in Indonesian; *nam katee* in Thai)
Is not the watery liquid that you can drink from a newly opened nut, but is the milk extracted from the flesh. It can easily be made from fresh grated coconut (that is how we make it in countries where coconuts and servants are plentiful), but in the West it is more conveniently made from dried coconut flakes. You can also purchase coconut milk in cans.

If you use fresh grated coconut, one nut will make about 2 cups of medium-thick milk. Pour hot water over the grated flesh and let it stand until lukewarm. Then press and squeeze the flesh to extract the milk, and pass through a sieve to separate the liquid. The more water you use, the thinner the milk will be; each recipe in this book will specify thick or thin coconut milk.

If you use dried coconut flakes, use 3/4 of a pound of dried coconut flakes and 2 cups of water to make a thick coconut milk, following one of the methods described below. To make a thin coconut milk, repeat the procedure again, using the same amount of water. By mixing the two extractions you will get a medium-thick coconut milk, which is the standard thickness for most dishes.

(1) Put the dried coconut into a blender and pour in 2 cups of water, which should be hot to the touch. Run the blender for 20–30 seconds, then pass the mush through a fine sieve, squeezing and pressing the coconut flakes as dry as you can. Put the coconut back into the blender, add more water, and repeat the blending and sieving.

(2) Put the dried coconut flakes in a saucepan, pour the water over it, bring to a boil, and simmer for 4–5 minutes. Allow to cool until hand-hot, then sieve and strain as described above.

Coconut milk (made from fresh or dried coconut) must be used while fresh. It can be stored briefly in the refrigerator about a day.

Coconut cream

Is the thick white liquid that separates and gathers at the surface if you refrigerate coconut milk. A few recipes specify the cream, and you simply spoon it off as required. If you want the milk, however, just stir the "cream" back into the clearer liquid on which it floats. Coconut cream can be purchased in cans.

CORIANDER SEEDS, CUMIN SEEDS

A few recipes call for these seeds to be roasted. Roast them on the stove. Spread a small quantity of the seeds in a frying pan and heat for a few minutes, shaking the pan or dish several times as if you were roasting almonds. When the seeds are ready, they will have darkened somewhat and there will be a strong, pleasant aroma.

DAIKON

This long white radish is readily available in supermarkets.

FERMENTED YELLOW OR BLACK BEANS

Indonesian, *tauco* (from the Chinese). These are used in dishes of Chinese origin and are easy to find, canned or dried, in Chinese shops.

FISH SAUCE

Thai, *nam pla*. This salty, savory, appetite-whetting sauce is used in a great many Thai dishes and has much the same function as soy sauce *(kecap)* in Indonesian cooking.

FLAT-LEAVED PARSLEY

This is also sometimes known as Italian parsley and differs from the more common curly parsley.

GALINGAL
(Languas galanga)

Indonesian, *laos;* Thai, *ka.* This is a rhizome or root, like ginger but with a somewhat mellower taste. Fresh galingal can be chopped like ginger, and the suggestions for the use of ginger (see below) apply to galingal as well. It is also available in dried form. If using a large piece of dried galingal, remember to take it out of the dish before serving. Galingal powder is also widely available.

GINGER
(Zingiber officinale)

If you like fresh ginger, put plenty in, chop it fine, and enjoy it. If you don't particularly want the gingery taste to come through, simply cut the ginger into two or three thick slices and remove them before the dish is served. If you really don't like ginger, use a little ground dried ginger instead. It will make its own small contribution to the overall effect.

KAFFIR LIME
(Citrus hystrix)

Indonesian, *jeruk purut;* Thai, *makrut.* This is a type of citrus fruit found in many parts of Southeast Asia. The dried leaves and rinds can be found in Asian shops. The leaves (*daun jeruk purut, bai makrut*) are used in Indonesia and Thailand; the rind (*piw makrut*) in Thailand only.

KECAP MANIS:
(see soy sauce)

LEMONGRASS
(Cymbopogon citratus)

Indonesian, *sereh;* Thai, *takrai.* This herb, which looks like a coarse grass, is used in many recipes for its mildly sour-sweet, citrus flavor. It can be bought, fresh or ground, in many Asian shops. It may sometimes be persuaded to grow as a house plant. It is sold in stems about 6 to 9 inches long, with the tough but fragrant outer leaves trimmed short. For most dishes, cut the stem into three equal pieces; one of these is usually sufficient. Remember to remove it before serving. For Thai curries and the Balinese "bumbu lengkap," the outer leaves are stripped off and only the tender heart is used, chopped into rounds like a scallion or put together with other spices to be blended into a smooth paste.

MUSTARD GREENS

You can buy these fresh in many health food stores and some supermarkets.

NOODLES

Indonesian and Thai, *mie* or *mee* (from the Chinese). There are many types, just as there are of pasta. Here are the ones you are most likely to come across.

Egg noodles (bakmie, ba mee)
Look much like spaghetti, except they are usually sold in tangled yellow blocks, not bunches of straight sticks. You can occasionally buy fresh ones, but the dried noodles in packages are really just as good and will keep for months. There are round ones and flat ones. These are made from eggs and wheat flour.

17

Rice vermicelli *(miehun, sen mee)*

Are very thin and sold in what looks like a skein of whitish wire. A thicker type are rice noodles, labeled "rice sticks"—these are like bundles of narrow white ribbon.

Bean threads *(biehun, woon sen)*

Are also called cellophane or clear noodles because they are colorless, almost transparent. These are also very thin. They are made from mung beans.

PALM SUGAR

Indonesian, *gula jawa, gula merah* or *gula melaka;* Thai, *nam tan peep.* This is brown sugar made from the juice of the coconut palm flower; it is sold in hard cakes, and you grate it, scrape it, or hack a piece off and crush it. Some shops call it by its Anglo-Burmese name, jaggery.

PANDAN
(Pandanus odorus, P. odoratissimus)

Indonesian, *pandan;* Thai, *bai toey hom.* Pandan leaves are used as a flavoring in desserts and as a green coloring. Bottled pandan is available in Asian markets.

PEANUTS
(Arachis hypogaea)

Indonesian, *kacang tanah;* Thai, *tooa.* Use raw, unsalted peanuts. They are used in Southeast Asia because they are cheap, filling, and nutritious. Like chiles, peanuts were brought from Central America to Southeast Asia. Today, you wonder how Asia ever managed without them. The use of peanut butter as a shortcut to saté sauce is not recommended, but it is possible.

RICE

As an Indonesian, I have to say that the best rice available in the West in Indonesian and Thai cooking is "Thai fragrant" rice. Although it may be described as "perfumed" on the bag, the only fragrance is a very pleasant smell of freshly cooked rice that wafts from the kitchen at dinner time. I always cook my rice in an electric steamer, using 1 1/4 cups of water to every cup of dry rice; this gives the rather moist, slightly sticky boiled rice that Indonesians like. If you prefer harder, separate grains, you can add a little less water or use Basmati or some other type.

Glutinous or "sticky" rice is used in Indonesia for making sweets, but it is also eaten as a main course. It is well worth trying. It is more filling than ordinary rice, so don't cook quite as much as you normally would.

If you don't have an electric rice cooker, rice is still very easy to boil: wash it well, and put it in a heavy saucepan with about twice its own volume of water. Don't put any salt in at any time. Bring the water to a boil, then simmer quietly, uncovered, until the rice has absorbed it all. Then cover the pan—even weigh the lid down—and continue cooking on low heat for 10 minutes. The layer of rice that sticks to the bottom should be thrown away (unless you like to deep-fry it, as Indonesians do, after it is thoroughly dry). If you have a double-saucepan steamer, steam the rice in it for the final 10 minutes (but note that steamed rice needs to absorb more water in the first stage of cooking—up to 1 1/2 times its own volume).

SALAM LEAF
(Eugenia polyantha)

Indonesian, *daun salam.* A single salam leaf is placed in the pan during cooking. Dried leaves are sold in most Asian markets. A bay leaf is a good substitute.

SAMBAL

This is the Indonesian word for hot chiles, crushed in salt, used both in cooking and as a condiment. You can make your own or buy it from Asian markets.

SHRIMPS, DRIED

Indonesian, *ebi.* These very tiny dried shrimps are available in specialty food shops. The shrimp are usually roasted before being packaged. Soak them in cold water for 10 minutes, then chop or put them in a blender.

SHRIMP PASTE

Indonesian, *terasi* (also spelled *trassie;* the names *balachan* and *blachen* are also used); Thai, *kapee* or *kapi.* This extremely pungent, salty, savory hard paste is used throughout Indonesia, Malaysia, and Thailand. Use it in small amounts. It keeps almost indefinitely. For a few recipes, the paste is grilled or fried before use. The fried or grilled shrimp paste can be crumbled so it can be measured with a teaspoon. "Raw" paste is crushed or blended along with other spices for dishes in which the spiced paste is then fried. Whatever you think of the smell (and some Westerners like it, when they get used to it), you will find that this condiment does great things for your savory dishes, so do use it. It is available in Asian markets.

SOM SA

Indonesian, *jeruk sambal.* These are very small green limes, even smaller than a kaffir lime. Ordinary limes can be used instead.

SOY SAUCE

Indonesian, *kecap*—pronounced, of course, "ketchup." This dark-colored, salty-tasting liquid has been produced from soybeans, by a complicated process of fermentation, for centuries. Any commercially available brand is perfectly good for any of the dishes in this book. Some recipes, however, specify light or dark soy, and there is a perceptible difference in taste. In general, light soy sauce is thinner and saltier, dark is thicker and sweeter. All soy sauces are strong-tasting and must be used sparingly; even the darkest contains a lot of salt. *Kecap manis* simply means "sweet" (i.e., dark) soy.

SPRING ROLL WRAPPERS

These are thin pastry squares which are essential for making spring rolls. They can be found in the freezer of specialty food shops. They come in several sizes; I use 5-inch and 8 1/2-inch squares. The pastry gets dry very easily, so the best way to use it is to thaw the whole package and peel the sheets off very carefully, one by one; you can then freeze them again. Once they have been separated they can be filled and rolled quickly and easily.

TAMARIND
(Tamarindus indica)

Indonesian, *asam* or *assem;* Thai, *mak kam.* Tamarind gives dishes the faint sourness that counteracts and provides depth to the

19

sweetness of much Southeast Asian food. Many of my recipes specify tamarind water, which is made by simmering a chunk of dried tamarind pulp in water for several minutes, letting it cool, and then squeezing and pressing it to extract the juices. Discard the remains of the pulp and put the dark-colored, unappetizing liquid in with the rest of the ingredients. It will taste good. If you use tamarind water often, it is worth making a small stock of it; it will keep in the refrigerator for at least a month. Put a whole 1-pound block into 4 cups of water and simmer until the liquid has reduced to half its volume. Then squeeze and sieve as above, and store the thick liquid in an airtight jar.

Whole tamarind pods are sold in Latin and Asian markets. The pulp inside the pods is pleasantly tart. Blocks of pulp are available in Indian and Asian stores. This form of tamarind is easier to use. Tamarind in liquid or powdered form is also available in Asian stores. Substitute fresh lemon juice if you like.

TEMPEH

Indonesian, *tempe*. Tempe is a block made from soybeans, cooked and then fermented with a special yeast or mold. This "digests" the part of the soybean that human beings cannot, so the full nutritional value of the beans is not only preserved but enhanced. When you slice tempeh you can see the individual beans, knitted together by the mold. It has a more interesting flavor and texture than tofu. It is becoming a well-known health food in North America. Don't eat tempeh if it is too old and smells of ammonia.

TOFU

Indonesian, *tahu*. This soft, cream-colored paste or gel is prepared from soybeans and is full of nutrients. It can be obtained almost everywhere in the U.S. Fresh tofu, which must

be refrigerated, submerged in water, will last for three to four days. Fried tofu is available in the refrigerator case along with fresh tofu. "Silken" tofu will keep for a year or more, even without refrigeration, provided the package is not opened; once open, it must be used within a day or two. It will do for cooking but is a bit runny.

WATER CHESTNUTS

These are easily obtainable in cans in specialty food stores.

WONTON WRAPPERS

These are squares of very thin pastry, like lasagna but much thinner. They measure about 3 inches each way. They can be purchased in supermarkets or specialty food shops.. They are necessary for making such Chinese delicacies as wontons. They can be bought either fresh or frozen, but their life in the refrigerator is limited to a few days. If you freeze them, pack them in small quantities and thaw them completely, peeling each one off the pile before using them. They dry out very quickly like filo and become brittle. You *can* make your own wrappers (1 1/4 cups flour, 2 eggs, salt, and cold water) in which case a pasta machine helps.

WOODEARS FUNGUS

These are sold in Chinese shops, often labeled "dried black fungus." At this stage they look neither appetizing nor edible, but a 30-minute soak in hot water makes them soft. They are delicious as part of the filling for a spring roll.

SOUPS AND STARTERS

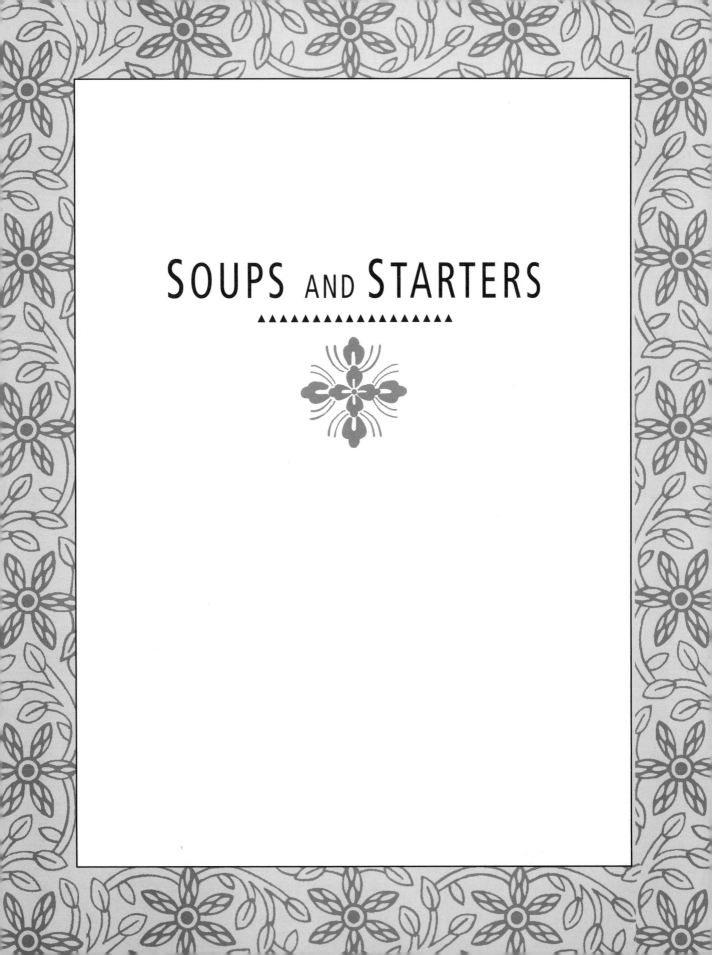

I've got used to the idea of starting off a dinner party with soup, even though in Indonesia and Thailand soup would be on the table all the way through the meal to wash the food down. We do not drink wine, and my grandmother did not even let us drink water during a meal, because water and rice, she said, would make us feel uncomfortably full, and we were supposed to enjoy her superb cooking. What I have found works for a dinner party is to start off with one or two dishes that are "dry" in the sense that they have little or no sauce. Only then do you have soup, so that it forms a kind of first-act finale.

Among the soups, soto, laksa and tom yam gung can represent Indonesia, Malaysia, and Thailand, respectively. On the drier side, saté is familiar in all three countries, as are spring rolls in one shape or another, even though they were originally Chinese. What all these dishes have in common is the way they exploit contrasts of taste and texture—the crunchy skin of the spring roll against the spicy smoothness of the sauce, or the different sensations you get from crab and young sweet corn when you bite into them.

Soup tureen, whole tamarind, tamarind slices, galingal, kaffir lime leaves, lemongrass cut in rounds, yard-long beans

Hot and Sour Soup with Fish

TOM SUM

SERVES 4–6

You can mix several kinds of fish in this recipe. Use whatever vegetables you like; I like green vegetables, such as mustard greens and watercress, mixed with daikon.

The stock should always be clear. The soup doesn't need to be too sour or too hot. The sourness comes from the tamarind. I often use a very good chicken stock and put in the juice of one lemon just before serving. What follows, however, is the authentic way of making hot and sour soup.

INGREDIENTS

4 cups cold water	2 cups chicken or vegetable stock or water (optional)
3 tamarind slices	1/2 pound mustard greens, shredded
2–4 fresh or dried chiles	1 bunch watercress
2 kaffir lime leaves or bay leaves	1/4 pound daikon, finely sliced
1 1-inch piece ginger	1 pound deboned fish fillets, cut into large pieces
1 1-inch fresh or dried galingal	3 tablespoons chopped cilantro
1 stalk fresh lemongrass, cut into 3 pieces	1 tablespoon light soy sauce
1 1/2 teaspoons salt	1 tablespoon fish sauce
1 tablespoon peanut oil	
1 medium onion, chopped	

METHOD

■ To make the stock, put the water into a large saucepan with the tamarind, chiles, kaffir lime leaves or bay leaves, ginger, galingal, lemongrass, and salt. Bring to a boil and simmer for 20–30 minutes. By this time the stock will be very fragrant from the lemongrass and other aromatic ingredients. Strain this through a fine sieve, discarding the solids.

■ In a large saucepan, heat the oil and fry the onion until soft, then add the stock you have just made. Simmer for 15 minutes. Add the chicken or vegetable stock or water, if desired (this additional liquid is needed if the soup is to serve 6 people). Add the mustard greens, watercress, and daikon. Simmer for 4 minutes. Increase the heat and bring the stock to a rolling boil, then add the fish and cilantro. Let the mixture boil for 4 minutes, then add the soy sauce and fish sauce. Cook the soup for 1 more minute, then serve immediately.

Hot and Sour Soup with Prawns

TOM YAM GUNG

SERVES 4–6

This is the most popular of the Thai hot and sour soups. The best hot and sour soups I have eaten in restaurants had plenty of prawns and only a small quantity of vegetables. The vegetables of choice are mustard greens and dried mushrooms. I use carrots and daikon, with a little mustard greens or watercress and dried mushrooms or, if I can get them, fresh oyster mushrooms.

INGREDIENTS

1 pound large prawns with shells	1 medium onion, chopped
1 teaspoon salt, divided	2 cups chicken or vegetable stock or water (optional)
4 cups cold water	
3 tamarind slices	2 medium carrots
2 kaffir lime leaves or bay leaves	1/4 pound daikon
2–4 fresh or dried chiles	1/4 pound shredded mustard greens or 1 bunch shredded watercress
1 1-inch piece ginger	
1 1-inch fresh or dried galingal	1/8 pound oyster mushrooms or 1 tablespoon woodears fungus
1 stalk fresh lemon grass, cut into 3 pieces	
1 tablespoon peanut oil	1 tablespoon fish auce

METHOD

■ Peel and devein the prawns. Wash the prawns and the shells thoroughly. Place the prawns on a plate, sprinkle with half the salt, and keep in the refrigerator until needed. Put the shells aside.

■ Put the water into a large saucepan with the tamarind, chiles, kaffir lime leaves or bay leaves, ginger, galingal, lemongrass, and the remaining salt. Bring to a boil and simmer for 20–30 minutes. By this time the stock will be very fragrant from the lemongrass and other aromatic ingredients.

■ In a small saucepan, heat the oil and fry the onion until soft, then add the prawn shells and stir for about 2 minutes. Add the onion and prawn shells, without any oil, into the stock. Continue to simmer for 15 minutes. Then strain the stock through a fine sieve into another large saucepan, discarding the solids. Add the chicken or vegetable stock or water, if desired (this additional liquid is needed if the soup is to serve 6 people). Set aside to reheat later.

METHOD

■ While the hot and sour stock is brewing, prepare the vegetables. Peel the carrots and daikon and cut them into thin rounds. If the daikon is very large, cut the rounds in half. Pick over and wash the mustard greens or watercress. Shred the oyster mushrooms. If using woodears fungus, soak them in boiling water for 30 minutes, then remove the stalks. Add the stalks and water to the stock. Slice the softened mushrooms.

■ Gently boil the strained stock. Add the carrots, daikon, and mushrooms. Simmer for 10 minutes. Increase the heat and bring the stock to a rolling boil, then add the prawns. Let the mixture boil for 3 minutes, then add the mustard greens or watercress and the fish sauce. Cook the soup for 1 more minute, then serve immediately.

Crabmeat and Baby Corn Soup

SUP KEPITING DENGAN JAGUNG MUDA

SERVES 4–6

I developed this soup at a hotel restaurant in London from a very simple recipe that we had often at home when I was young. It is a sweet soup, which is very refreshing, especially since in Indonesia we eat soup throughout a spicy meal.

INGREDIENTS

1 tablespoon sunflower oil	2 teaspoons light soy sauce
6 shallots, thinly sliced	2 cups chicken stock
1 tablespoon sugar	1/2 pound crabmeat (white meat only), fresh, frozen, or canned
1/2 pound frozen, thawed baby sweet corn, thinly sliced	1/4 pound fried tofu, thinly sliced
pinch cayenne	3 tablespoons chopped Italian parsley
3 large slices ginger	3 tablespoons thinly sliced scallions or chives
salt to taste	

METHOD

■ In a saucepan, heat the oil and fry the shallots for 2 minutes. Add the sugar and stir continuously for another 2 minutes. Add the baby corn, stir, and add the cayenne, ginger, salt, and soy sauce. Add the stock, then bring to a boil and simmer for 25–30 minutes. Taste, and add more salt, if necessary.

■ Stir in the crabmeat, tofu, parsley, and scallions or chives and simmer for 3–5 minutes. Discard the ginger slices before serving hot.

Prawn and Vermicelli Soup

LAKSA LEMAK

SERVES 4–6

Laksa Lemak is really the Malaysian name for soto (soup) made with noodles and coconut milk. The Indonesians have adopted the name because an explanatory name in Indonesian would be very long. You will certainly find Laksa Lemak on restaurant menus in Malaysia and Singapore as well as Indonesia.

INGREDIENTS

1/4 pound pork fillet or chicken breast	1 2-inch piece ginger
salt and pepper to taste	1 teaspoon ground coriander
2 cups water	1/2 teaspoon turmeric
1/2 pound prawns with shells	3 cups thick coconut milk
1/2 pound rice vermicelli	4 thick slices fried tofu
1 1/2 teaspoons vegetable oil	1/4 pound bean sprouts
5 shallots, thinly sliced	4–5 scallions, thinly sliced
2 cloves garlic, crushed	

METHOD

■ Boil the pork or chicken, seasoned with salt and pepper, in the water for 45 minutes. Drain the meat, reserving the stock, and slice into small, thin pieces. Clean the prawns and discard the heads.

■ Put the vermicelli into a saucepan and add enough boiling water to cover. Cover the pan and let it sit for 5 minutes. Then strain off the water.

■ Heat the oil in a wok or a deep saucepan and sauté the shallots for 1 minute. Add the garlic, ginger, coriander, and turmeric. Stir for another half-minute, then add the meat. Stir for 1 more minute, add the stock, and simmer for 25 minutes.

■ Add the vermicelli and the coconut milk and continue to simmer very gently. When the coconut milk starts to boil, stir gently to prevent it from curdling.

■ Add the prawns, tofu, and bean sprouts and simmer for another 5 minutes, stirring occasionally. Just before serving, add the scallions. Serve hot.

Madura Beef Soup

SOTO MADURA

**SERVES 6-8
AS A STARTER**

Many people think that this dish should be made with chicken. There certainly are other kinds of soto that use chicken, but Soto Madura should have beef; after all, the island from which it takes its name is famous for its buffalo. It is good served as part of an elaborate dinner or by itself.

INGREDIENTS

1 pound boned beef brisket, trimmed	1 1-inch piece ginger
5 cups water	1/4 teaspoon turmeric
salt and pepper to taste	3 shallots, minced
2 tablespoons corn oil, divided	1/2 teaspoon cayenne (optional)
4 candlenuts or raw macadamia nuts, chopped	4 tablespoons bean sprouts (optional)
1 onion, chopped	1 tablespoon minced Italian parsley
3 cloves garlic, chopped	1 tablespoon fried shallots or onion
1/4 pound prawns with shells, chopped	4 lemon slices

METHOD

■ Put the beef into a large saucepan, cover with the water, and add a little salt and pepper. Bring to a boil, cover, and simmer for 1 hour 15 minutes, skimming the surface all the time.

■ Remove the meat from the pan, and strain the stock through a fine sieve into a bowl. Set the stock aside. Cut the meat into small cubes, discarding any fat or gristle.

■ Heat 1 tablespoon of the oil in a saucepan, and fry the candlenuts or macadamia nuts, onion, garlic, and prawns for 1 minute. Add the ginger, turmeric, and half the meat stock. Cover and simmer for 15 minutes.

■ Fry the shallots in a large pan until they are golden brown, using the remaining oil. Add the beef, 4 tablespoons of the stock, a pinch of salt, and the cayenne, if desired. Cover and simmer for 2 minutes.

■ Strain the liquid in which the prawns and candlenuts or macadamia nuts were cooked into the pan that contains the beef. Put in the rest of the stock. Bring to a boil, lower the heat, cover, and simmer for 20–25 minutes. If bean sprouts are used, put them in just before you serve the soup. Garnish with parsley, fried shallots, and lemon slices.

Steamed Spring Rolls

POPIA SOHT

MAKES ABOUT 20 SPRING ROLLS

These spring rolls are normally filled with minced pork, prawns, bamboo shoots, and bean sprouts. However, for steamed spring rolls, I prefer a vegetarian version: after all, they are called "spring" rolls because originally they were filled with spring vegetables. Like the miniature fried spring rolls, these are served in Thai restaurants as a starter.

INGREDIENTS

1/8 pound package of cellophane noodles	2 tablespoons rinsed and chopped woodears fungus, first soaked in hot water for 4 minutes
2 tablespoons vegetable oil	
1 pound carrots, cut into tiny matchsticks	5 scallions, thinly sliced
1/2 pound string beans, cut into thin rounds	1 1/2-inch piece ginger, chopped
1/4 pound cabbage, very finely shredded	2 tablespoons light soy sauce
1/2 pound canned bamboo shoots, cut into tiny matchsticks	1 egg, separated
1 teaspoon salt	1 package of 20 spring roll wrappers (8 1/2 inches square)
1 1/2 teaspoon ground white pepper	

METHOD

■ To make the filling, soak the noodles in hot water for 3 minutes, drain, and chop. Heat the oil in a wok or frying pan and stir-fry the carrots first, then the beans, cabbage, and bamboo shoots. Season with the salt and pepper. After 4 minutes of stir-frying, add the noodles, woodears fungus, scallions, ginger, and soy sauce. Continue stirring for another 2 minutes. Taste, and adjust the seasoning. Let cool. When cool, mix the egg yolk thoroughly into the filling (the white will be used later to seal the rolls).

■ Place a wrapper on a flat surface (e.g. a plate or tray), and put about 2 tablespoons of the filling onto one corner. Pull the corner over the filling and roll up the wrapper with the filling inside it. Then fold the two side flaps towards the center, brush the remaining flap with egg white, and fold it up so that the roll is sealed. Repeat the process until all the rolls are made and sealed. Arrange them in a single layer on a plate and steam them for 4–5 minutes. Serve hot as a starter with Sweet and Sour Chile Sauce (page 145).

Fried Miniature Spring Rolls

POPIA TAWT

MAKES 50 SPRING ROLLS

Miniature spring rolls are normally served as a starter in Thai restaurants. They are similar to Indonesian lumpia, but not as big. I have served them hundreds of times as finger food at cocktail parties, or as a first course. Although I always make the filling, I delegate the job of rolling them to my Philippine friend who makes all the rolls exactly the same size and equally perfect. You can vary the filling, using prawns with pork, chicken, or crabmeat, or you can have a vegetable filling. Here is my favorite, prawn and crabmeat, using the white meat only.

These ingredients will make about 50 miniature spring rolls. The wrappers can be bought in supermarkets, usually from the freezer section.

INGREDIENTS

1 package of 50 spring roll wrappers (5 inches square)

1/4 pound package cellophane noodles

1/2 pound uncooked prawns without shells

1/4 pound crabmeat (white meat only)

4 carrots, cut into tiny matchsticks

1/4 pound cabbage, shredded

2 tablespoons rinsed and chopped woodears fungus, first soaked in hot water for 4 minutes

5 scallions, thinly sliced

2 cloves garlic, crushed

1 1/2-inch piece ginger, minced

1/2 teaspoon cayenne

1 teaspoon salt

1 tablespoon light soy sauce

1 egg, separated

vegetable oil for frying

crispy lettuce leaves

sweet and sour chile sauce (page 145)

METHOD

■ Assuming the wrappers are bought frozen, thaw them out completely and carefully peel each one from the pile. Then cover them with a towel to prevent them from drying.

■ To make the filling, soak the noodles in hot water for 3 minutes, drain, and chop. In a large bowl mix together the noodles with the remaining ingredients except the egg, oil, lettuce, and chile sauce. Mix the egg yolk thoroughly into the filling (the white will be used later to seal the rolls).

METHOD

■ Place a wrapper on a flat surface (e.g. a plate or tray), and put about 2 teaspoons of the filling onto the corner nearest you. Pull the corner over the filling and roll up the wrapper with the filling inside it, but leave the corner furthest from you free, like the flap of an envelope. Then fold the two side flaps towards the center, brush the remaining flap with egg white, and fold it so that the roll is sealed. Repeat the process until all the rolls are made and sealed.

■ Deep-fry the rolls, 6 or 8 at a time, in hot oil until golden brown and crisp. To eat, wrap each one in a lettuce leaf, then dip it into the sauce.

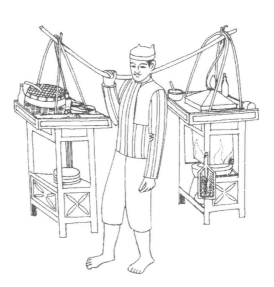

Ground Pork Saté Balinese-Style

SATÉ LILIT

MAKES 12-16 SATÉ

Don't be put off by the long list of spices. The result is well worth the trouble. The Balinese call this combination of spices *bumbu lengkap* (a complete set of spices); it is also used for Ayam Betutu (page 78) and Saté Bebek (page 34).

INGREDIENTS

4 shallots	1/2 teaspoon white pepper
2 cloves garlic	1 2-inch stalk lemongrass or 1/2 teaspoon lemongrass powder
5 red chiles, seeded, or 1 teaspoon cayenne	thin slice shrimp paste (about 2 inches square) (optional)
5 tablespoons very thick coconut milk	2 tablespoons water
3 teaspoons coriander seeds	4 tablespoons vegetable oil, divided
2 teaspoons cumin seeds	1 tablespoon salt
2 cloves	1 pound ground pork
1 2-inch cinnamon stick	juice of 1 lime
1/2 teaspoon ground nutmeg	12–16 6-inch bamboo saté sticks
1/2 teaspoon turmeric	
1/2 teaspoon galingal	

METHOD

■ To make the spice mixture, put all the ingredients except 2 tablespoons of the oil, the pork, lime juice, and saté sticks in a food processor and process until smooth. (Use a pestle and mortar if you prefer.) Fry this paste in the remaining 2 tablespoons oil, stirring continuously, for about 5 minutes, or until the smell of raw shallots and garlic has been replaced by a pleasant spicy fragrance. Add the salt, and let cool.

■ When the paste is cool, mix it in a bowl with the pork. Knead with your hand for a while, then add the lime juice and mix again. Cover and chill for 1–2 hours.

METHOD

■ Divide the meat mixture into 12–16 portions. Form each portion into a ball, then put the bamboo stick in the middle and with your hand form the meatball into a small sausage shape around the stick. Repeat this process until you have 12–16 sticks of saté.

■ Grill the saté under a grill or electric broiler lined with aluminum foil or on a charcoal barbecue for 10–12 minutes, carefully turning the sticks over several times. Or you can cook them in the oven at 350°F for 30–35 minutes, turning once.

■ Serve hot for lunch with a salad or as a first course. They are also good for cocktail parties. As they are already quite spicy, no other sauce is necessary.

Duck Saté Balinese-Style

SATÉ BEBEK

SERVES 4

As with Saté Lilit (page 32), the marinade is the Balinese *bumbu lengkap*. From experience I can recommend this duck saté with no hesitation. However, it is quite expensive because we use the fillet of duck breast only.

INGREDIENTS

4 duck breasts, quartered	1 2-inch cinnamon stick
1 tablespoon salt	1/2 teaspoon ground nutmeg
juice of 1 lime	1/2 teaspoon turmeric
8 8-inch bamboo saté sticks	1/2 teaspoon galingal
4 shallots, chopped	1/2 teaspoon white pepper
2 cloves garlic	1 2-inch stalk lemongrass or 1/2 teaspoon lemongrass powder
5 red chiles, seeded, or 1 teaspoon cayenne	
5 tablespoons very thick coconut milk	thin slice shrimp paste (about 2 inches square) (optional)
3 teaspoons coriander seeds	1 tablespoon salt
2 teaspoons cumin seeds	4 tablespoons vegetable oil, divided
2 cloves	2 tablespoons water

METHOD

■ Cut each duck breast into 4 pieces, leaving the skin. Rub the pieces with the salt and lime juice. Set aside while preparing the spice paste.

■ To make the spice paste, put the remaining ingredients except 2 tablespoons of the oil into a food processor and process until smooth. Fry this paste in the remaining 2 tablespoons of oil, stirring continuously, for about 5 minutes. Add the salt, and let cool.

■ When the paste is cool, mix it thoroughly with the duck. Then put 4 pieces of meat onto each bamboo stick, and marinate for at least 2 hours or in the refrigerator overnight.

■ Grill the saté under a gas or electric broiler lined with aluminum foil or on a charcoal barbecue for 10–12 minutes, turning several times, making sure that the skin is crisp. Or you can cook them skin side up in the oven 400°F for 30–35 minutes.

■ Serve hot for lunch with a salad or as a first course. These are also good for cocktail parties, with each piece of meat served on a cocktail stick. As they are already quite spicy, no other sauce is necessary.

Spicy Mushroom Cups

PEPES JAMUR

SERVES 4

On a recent visit to Yogyakarta I ate this dish almost every day. It was usually made with jamur merang—straw mushrooms which people grow themselves or buy in the marketplace. The canned straw mushrooms that are available in the West are fine, but fresh mushrooms are best, either cultivated or wild.

INGREDIENTS

1 pound mushrooms, sliced	2 shallots, finely sliced
1/2 teaspoon salt	2 tablespoons chopped chives
1/2 cup coconut cream (see page 2)	2 tablespoons chopped mint
2 green chiles, seeded	1 egg

METHOD

- Spread the mushrooms on a plate and sprinkle with the salt.

- Mix the coconut cream with all the other ingredients in a bowl. Taste, and add more salt, if necessary.

- In Indonesia this mixture is wrapped in banana leaves and steamed for 10 minutes, to be eaten hot or cold as a snack. Another easy alternative is to divide the mushroom mixture among 4 cups or ramekins, and steam them; or bake them in the oven at 350°F in a water bath for 10–15 minutes. Serve as a first course with thin slices of bread and butter or buttered toast.

Stuffed Squid

CUMI-CUMI ISI

SERVES 6–8

Both the Indonesians and the Thais love squid. This one is an Indonesian recipe, which normally has a chile-hot stuffing. But it is also good without chile.

INGREDIENTS

2 pounds medium squid	1/2 teaspoon cayenne
1 large potato	1 teaspoon salt
4 carrots	2 large eggs
2 tablespoons vegetable oil	1/2 cup water
5 shallots or 1 onion, minced	2 tablespoons chopped Italian parsley
3 cloves garlic, minced	4 tablespoons chopped scallions
1 1/2-inch piece ginger, minced	1/2 cup tamarind water, seasoned with salt and pepper
1 teaspoon ground coriander	

METHOD

■ Clean the squid thoroughly, discarding the ink sacs. Chop the tentacles to mix with the stuffing.

■ To make the stuffing, cut the potato and carrots into very small cubes (less than 1/4 inch). Keep the potato cubes in salted water to prevent them from discoloring.

■ In a wok or shallow saucepan, heat the oil. Fry the shallots or onion and garlic until soft, and add the carrots. Stir, then add the ginger, coriander, cayenne, and salt. Stir almost continuously for about 3 minutes. Drain the potato, stir in, then add the water. Cover and simmer for 3 minutes.

■ Uncover, add the chopped tentacles, and continue cooking for another 3 minutes, stirring frequently. Taste, adding salt, if necessary. When the vegetables are soft, remove the pan from the heat and allow to cool. Beat in the eggs, mixing thoroughly.

■ Use this mixture to stuff the squid, but don't fill each squid too full. Close the opening with toothpicks. Arrange the squid in a baking dish, which should fit inside your steamer. (Or you can cook the squid in the oven.)

METHOD Sprinkle the parsley and scallions over the squid and pour on the seasoned tamarind water. Put the dish into the steamer and steam for 1 hour (or cook in a medium oven for the same time).

■ There will be quite a lot of juice in the dish when you finish steaming. Pour this sauce into a small saucepan, and boil to reduce by half.

■ Let cool a little before removing the toothpicks, then slice the squid. Serve hot or cold, with the sauce poured over.

Eggs Stuffed with Prawns and Crabmeat

KHAI KWAN

**SERVES 4
AS A FIRST
COURSE**

The real meaning of Khai Kwan is "precious egg" or "gift egg." Khai Kwan can be eaten hot or cold as a first course with green salad. They can also be served with drinks before the meal. Cut each egg into 4 pieces with a sharp knife that has been wet with hot water. If you have plenty of time, try making them with quail eggs—they are even more precious that way.

INGREDIENTS

4 large hard-boiled eggs	1 tablespoon fish sauce
4 large prawns without shells	4–5 tablespoons thick coconut milk
4 tablespoons cooked crabmeat	1/3 cup all-purpose flour
1 tablespoon cilantro, chopped	2/3 cup warm water
2 cloves garlic, chopped	1 tablespoon vegetable oil
freshly ground black pepper	1/4 teaspoon salt
1/2 teaspoon salt	vegetable oil for deep-frying

METHOD

■ To make the filling, peel and halve the eggs. Scrape out the yolks and put them in a bowl. Mince the prawns and mix them with crabmeat, cilantro, garlic, pepper, salt, and fish sauce. Add this mixture to the yolks in the bowl, mixing and mashing them with a fork. Add the coconut milk, a spoonful at a time, until the mixture is well blended and moist. You may find you need less than 5 tablespoons of coconut milk.

■ Divide the filling into 8 equal portions and put each portion into the half of an egg white, piling up the filling and shaping it so that you end up with 8 stuffed eggs.

■ To make the batter, put the flour, water, oil, and salt in a bowl, and beat until smooth.

■ Dip each of the stuffed eggs in the batter and deep-fry in hot oil for about 3 minutes, or until golden brown, keeping the filling upside down while frying. Take each egg out with a slotted spoon and drain on paper towels.

FISH AND SHELLFISH

▲▲▲▲▲▲▲▲▲▲▲▲▲▲▲▲▲▲▲

Indonesians sometimes refer to their country simply as tanah air—land and water. Less picturesquely, anyone who has ever been caught in a tropical downpour in Jakarta or Bangkok when there are no taxis in sight will appreciate how much water can fall from the sky in a few minutes. Indonesia, with its 13,000 islands, has an enormously long coastline.

Thailand is a more landlocked country, but it is seamed and threaded by networks of rivers. Both countries depend on rice as their basic food supply, so that irrigation systems, canals, reservoirs, and storage tanks are part of the landscape almost everywhere you go. With so much water, fresh and salt, it would be astonishing if Thais and Indonesians were anything less than great fish cooks. Fortunately, most of our favorite fish, or very acceptable substitutes, can be found easily in Western markets.

Thai boats in fish market

Spicy Steamed Scallops

TIRAM KUKUS

SERVES 4

You can steam the scallops in their shells or in little dishes or ramekins. I like my scallops quite spicy but plain, garnished with just a few chopped chives.

INGREDIENTS

8 scallops, cleaned, with roe	pinch ground coriander
1 clove garlic, crushed	2 tablespoons light soy sauce
1 green chile, seeded and minced	2 tablespoons water
1 small piece ginger, minced	1 tablespoon chopped chives
1 tablespoon vegetable oil	

METHOD

▪ Place 2 scallops on each shell or dish.

▪ In a wok or large frying pan, fry the garlic, chile, and ginger in the oil, stirring continuously, for 1 minute. Add the coriander, soy sauce, and water. Simmer for 2 minutes. Strain, and discard the ginger and chile. Spoon this spiced liquid on the scallops. Sprinkle the scallops with chives, and steam for 3–4 minutes. Serve immediately.

Scallop and Quail Egg Sambal Goreng

SAMBAL GORENG TIRAM DAN TELUR PUYUH

SERVES 4

"Sambal goreng" is a generic name for dishes found all over Indonesia. The best known dish is Sambal Goreng Udang (Prawn Sambal Goreng). This combination of scallops and quail eggs was suggested to me. It turned out so well that I have made it many times. Remember that scallops need very little cooking, so don't put them into the sauce more than 4 minutes before serving.

INGREDIENTS

4 shallots	1 tablespoon tamarind water or 1 tamarind slice
1 clove garlic	1 to 1 1/2 cups thick coconut milk
3 large red chiles, seeded, or pinch cayenne and 1 teaspoon paprika	1/2 stalk lemongrass or pinch lemongrass powder
2 candlenuts or raw macadamia nuts (optional)	2 kaffir lime leaves or bay leaves
1 1-inch slice shrimp paste	salt to taste
1 1-inch piece ginger	8 scallops, cleaned, with roe separated
4 tablespoons olive oil, divided	12 quail eggs, boiled for 3 minutes and peeled
2 tablespoons water	1 tomato, peeled, seeded, and chopped
1 teaspoon ground coriander	
pinch galingal	

METHOD

■ To make the sauce, put the shallots, garlic, chiles or cayenne and paprika, candlenuts or macadamia nuts, if desired, shrimp paste, ginger, 2 tablespoons of the oil, and water in a blender, and blend until smooth. Add the coriander and galingal to this paste.

■ Heat the remaining oil in a saucepan. Take the paste out of the blender and fry it, stirring continuously, for 2 minutes. Add the tamarind water or tamarind slice, stir, and add the coconut milk, lemongrass, and kaffir lime leaves or bay leaves. Bring to a boil, then reduce the heat and simmer, stirring frequently, for 50 minutes, or until the sauce thickens.

■ Adjust the seasoning. Take out the tamarind slice, if used, and the lemongrass. Just before you are ready to serve, heat the sauce to a rolling boil, add the scallops and roe, quail eggs, and tomato. Let this bubble gently for 4 minutes. Serve hot immediately. Do not reheat.

Stir-Fried Crab with Egg

ORAK-ARIK KEPITING

SERVES 4

This is a simple but very enjoyable dish that my mother cooked one day when I was in high school. I remember the day well—it was a rainy Sunday. My father, whose hobby was cooking, came back from the market with several live crabs. One of them tried to escape into the courtyard outside our kitchen, which was half-flooded by the rain. I caught it and gave it to my father, with my eyes closed because I hated to watch the live crabs being plunged into the big pot of boiling water. However, I forgot this soon enough when the dish my father cooked was put on the table. It was out of this world. Its name has gone completely from my memory. It was much too complicated for a 14-year-old girl who didn't have the slightest interest in cooking.

This, then, is what my mother made later, from the leftover white meat of the crabs—and it's very good , too.

INGREDIENTS

2 tablespoons coconut oil or peanut oil	1 tablespoon light soy sauce
4 shallots, minced	2 eggs, beaten
1 1-inch piece ginger, minced	1/2 teaspoon ground coriander
2 cloves garlic, minced	pinch cayenne
1/2–3/4 pound carrots or celery root, grated or cut into fine julienne sticks	salt to taste
1/2 pound crabmeat (white meat only)	3 tablespoons chopped Italian parsley or chives

METHOD

■ In a wok or large frying pan, heat the oil. Fry the shallots, ginger, and garlic for 2 minutes, stirring continuously. Add the carrots or celery root and continue to stir-fry for 3–4 minutes, or until the vegetables are tender. Then add the crabmeat and the soy sauce, and stir again for 1-2 minutes.

■ Season the eggs with the coriander, cayenne, and salt, and add them to the pan. Keep stirring and turning the mixture until the scrambled egg is well mixed with the crab and the vegetables. Stir in the parsley or chives just before serving hot with a main course of rice or noodles.

Prawns in Sweet and Sour Sauce

PRIEW WAN GUNG

This is another popular Thai restaurant dish which is simple to make at home. Just for a change, I have substituted tomatoes for tamarind in the sauce, but of course you can use tamarind water if you prefer.

INGREDIENTS

1 pound medium uncooked prawns without shells and heads	2 shallots, finely sliced
1 teaspoon salt	pinch cayenne
1 medium green bell pepper (optional)	1 tablespoon fish sauce
2 tomatoes	1 tablespoon light soy sauce
2 cloves garlic	2 teaspoons rice vinegar
1 1-inch piece ginger	1 tablespoon sugar
1 cup water	2 tablespoons chopped cilantro
1/4 teaspoon corn flour (optional)	2 scallions, thinly sliced
1/2 cup peanut oil	salt and sugar to taste

METHOD

■ Wash the prawns thoroughly. Drain and pat dry with paper towels. Sprinkle with the salt.

■ To make the sauce, if you are using the pepper cut it into julienne strips and blanch quickly in boiling water. Put the tomatoes, garlic, ginger, and water in a small saucepan. Boil vigorously for 4 minutes—the water will be much reduced by then. Pass the contents of the pan through a sieve into a bowl, crushing the tomatoes and garlic, so that you end up with several table-spoons of thick, garlicky, gingery tomato sauce. Set this aside to cool. When cool, if you are using corn flour, put it into this sauce.

■ In a wok or frying pan, heat the oil and fry the prawns in 2 batches for 3 minutes each time. Remove with a slotted spoon and drain in a colander.

■ Discard the oil, except for about 1 1/2 tablespoons. Heat this and fry the shallots until soft. Add the cayenne, fish sauce, soy sauce, vinegar, and sugar. Stir, and add the tomato sauce. Stir again, simmer for 1 minute, increase the heat, and add the prawns and pepper, f desired.

■ Stir continuously for another minute and add the cilantro and scallions. Continue cooking and stirring for 1 minute longer. Taste, and add salt and sugar, if necessary. Serve immediately.

Prawns with Pineapple

UDANG NENAS

SERVES 4

At home in Indonesia, this dish always brought me many compliments, probably because I used the best and freshest prawns I could find. When I got to England, I included the recipe as part of my entry for a wine-and-food menu competition. Not being a great wine connoisseur myself, I overlooked the fact that pineapple doesn't go well with fine wines, so I didn't win. But it goes extremely well with prawns.

Serve this as a starter, followed by a sweet soup such as Sup Kepiting Dengan Jagung Muda/Crabmeat and Baby Corn Soup (page 26). You will be ready then to enjoy the wine with the next course.

INGREDIENTS

16–20 large uncooked prawns, peeled and deveined	2 2/3 tablespoons olive oil, divided
salt, divided	1/2 cup + 2 tablespoons water
1 medium pineapple	pinch cayenne
3 shallots	1 tablespoon white malt vinegar
2 cloves garlic	2 teaspoons sugar
4 candlenuts or raw macadamia nuts	2 tablespoons chopped mint
1 1/2-inch piece ginger	

METHOD

■ Wash the prawns thoroughly. Drain and pat dry with paper towels. Sprinkle with 1 teaspoon salt.

■ Peel the pineapple. Core and discard the eyes. Then cut the fruit into small cubes. Put in a colander and sprinkle liberally with salt. Leave for 10 minutes, then rinse thoroughly under cold running water to wash the salt away.

■ To make the sauce, blend the shallots, garlic, candlenuts or macadamia nuts, and ginger with 2 teaspoons of the oil and 2 tablespoons of the water until smooth. Put the remaining oil in a wok or large frying pan, heat, and fry the paste, stirring continuously, for 2 minutes. Add cayenne, vinegar, and sugar. Stir, and add the remaining water. Simmer for 3 minutes, then adjust the seasoning.

■ Bring the sauce to a rolling boil and add the prawns. Stir, and let it bubble gently for 3 minutes. Add the pineapple cubes and mint and continue cooking, stirring constantly, for 2 minutes. Serve hot or cold.

45

Mixed Shellfish in Rich Coconut Milk Sauce

HOMOK TALAY

SERVES 4

The flavors in this dish are exquisite and spicy, full of mint and sweet basil and lemongrass. All the sea delicacies need very little cooking, so put them into the sauce just a few minutes before serving.

INGREDIENTS

8 scallops with the roe	3 cups very thick coconut milk, divided
8 large prawns with heads	3 cardamom seeds
8–12 mussels	2 tablespoons tamarind water or 2 tamarind slices
8 crab claws	
2 large squid without tentacles	2 kaffir lime leaves or bay leaves
3 large red chiles, seeded and chopped	1 teaspoon salt
4 shallots, chopped	1 teaspoon sugar
3 cloves garlic	handful mint leaves
1 1-inch piece ginger	handful basil leaves
1 2-inch stalk lemongrass, outer leaves discarded	2 tablespoons chopped cilantro (optional)

METHOD

■ Clean the scallops, separate the roe, and cut the white part in half. Remove the legs from the prawns, and wash thoroughly. Scrub the mussels well under cold running water, then boil in water for 1 minute. Leave them in the hot water for a few more minutes, then rinse under cold water to get rid of the sand that might remain inside the shell. Cut the squid into bite-size pieces, wash and boil in salted water for 5–6 minutes. Drain.

■ To make the sauce, put the chiles, shallots, garlic, ginger, and lemongrass into a blender, add 3 tablespoons of the coconut milk, and blend until you have a very smooth paste. Then put another 4 tablespoons of the coconut milk into a saucepan. Heat, and when boiling stir with a wooden spoon and add the paste from the blender. Stir again, and let simmer for 1–2 minutes.

■ Add the cardamom seeds, tamarind water or slices, kaffir lime leaves or bay leaves, salt, and sugar. Once again stir and add the rest of the coconut milk. Continue cooking and let this sauce bubble gently for 30–40 minutes, stirring frequently to prevent curdling, or until reduced by half.

■ Add the seafood, mint, basil, and cilantro, if desired, and continue cooking for 4–5 minutes. Taste, adjust the seasoning, remove the cardamom seeds and kaffir lime leaves or bay leaves, and serve immediately.

Fried Squid and Vegetables with Fish Sauce

PUD PLA MUEK

SERVES 4

This is a very popular dish in Thai restaurants, where chefs sometimes, in their desire to be authentic, use too much lemongrass and cilantro. The result is that you can scarcely taste anything else. I make this dish at home with a milder sauce, and the flavors are much subtler. The Thais are fond, too, of pickled garlic, which suits this dish very well.

INGREDIENTS

1 1/2 pounds small squid with tentacles	pinch cayenne
2 tablespoons tamarind water or juice of 1 lime	2 tablespoons fish sauce
1 teaspoon salt	1 teaspoon sugar
1 pound mustard greens	1 cup vegetable oil
1 1/2-inch slice pickled ginger	1 tablespoon chopped cilantro
1 clove pickled garlic	2 green chiles, seeded and chopped (optional)
pinch galingal	salt to taste
pinch lemongrass powder	

METHOD

■ Clean the squid thoroughly, discarding the head and ink sac. Chop the tentacles and slice the squid into small strips about 1/2 inch by 1 inch. Marinate these in the tamarind water or lime juice and salt for 40 minutes to an hour. Then drain and pat dry with paper towels.

■ To make the sauce, clean and roughly chop the mustard greens. Mince the pickled ginger and garlic or mash them with a pestle and mortar. Add the galingal, lemongrass, cayenne, fish sauce, and sugar. Mix well.

■ In a wok or frying pan heat the oil, and when really hot fry the squid in 2 or 3 batches for 3–4 minutes each time. Remove with a slotted spoon and drain in a colander.

■ When all the squid is fried, discard almost all the oil, leaving the wok or frying pan only slightly oily. Heat again, and when smoke starts to rise, add the cilantro and chiles, if desired, stirring well, then the mustard greens. Stir and turn vigorously for 2 minutes. Add salt, stir again, then add the sauce and continue stirring while you add the fried squid. Mix well, taste, adjust the seasoning, and serve immediately.

Squid Salad

YAM PLA MUEK

SERVES 4

Prepare the squid as you would for Pud Pla Muek/Fried Squid and Vegetables with Fish Sauce (page 47). Alternatively, for this typical Thai salad, instead of frying the squid you can boil it with a little salt for a fairly long time—maybe as long as an hour or more. If you boil it for 4–5 minutes, the chances are you will get a tender squid; cooking it for 15–20 minutes will make it tough and rubbery. But if you cook it longer still—say, an hour and a half—it goes tender again.

INGREDIENTS

juice of 2 limes	1 clove garlic, crushed (optional)
1 tablespoon fish sauce	1 tablespoon minced cilantro or Italian parsley
1 tablespoon sugar	
1 green chile, seeded and minced	1 1/2 pounds cooked squid
1 1/2-inch stalk lemongrass, soft inner part only, minced	

METHOD

■ To make the dressing, combine all the ingredients except the squid in a bowl. Mix well. Pour the dressing over the squid.

Fried Fish in Tamarind Sauce

IKAN ASAM MANIS

SERVES 4

For best results the sour and sweet sauce for this recipe should be made of tamarind water spiced with cayenne, garlic, and ginger.

INGREDIENTS

2 tablespoons white malt vinegar	1 2-inch piece ginger, chopped
2 cloves garlic, crushed	2 cloves garlic, chopped
1 teaspoon salt	2 teaspoons brown sugar
1 teaspoon ground coriander	1/2 teaspoon cayenne
1/2 teaspoon turmeric	1 teaspoon salt
4 red snappers, cleaned	4 scallions, thinly sliced
2 ounces tamarind pulp	vegetable oil for frying
2 cups water	2 tablespoons sliced gherkins
2 tablespoons olive oil	2 tablespoons chopped basil or mint

METHOD

■ To make the marinade, mix together the vinegar, garlic, salt, coriander, and turmeric. Rub all over the fish and marinate for 1 hour in the refrigerator.

■ Meanwhile, make the sauce. Dissolve the tamarind pulp in the water, then rub it through a sieve. Boil the liquid in a small saucepan until the quantity is reduced by half. In a frying pan or wok, heat the oil, and sauté the ginger and garlic for a few seconds. Add the sugar, cayenne, salt, and scallions, and stir. Stir in the thick tamarind water and adjust the seasoning.

■ Fry the fish in hot oil for about 5 minutes each side, turning them over once. Put the fish on a serving dish, heat the sauce quickly, and pour it over the fish. Garnish with gherkins and basil or mint. Serve immediately.

Sea Bass in Sweet and Sour Sauce with Mangoes

IKAN KUKUS DENGAN MANGGA

SERVES 4–6

Half-ripe mangoes are often used in salads and sauces—partly because mango trees grow in almost everyone's backyard in Indonesia. This dish will always make a big impression at any dinner party, whatever country you are in. You can use any white-fleshed fish instead of sea bass.

INGREDIENTS

1 3 1/2-pound sea bass, cleaned and gutted	3 candlenuts or raw macadamia nuts
1/2 teaspoon salt	1 tablespoon wine vinegar
juice of 1 lime	2 tablespoons olive oil, divided
1/2 stalk lemongrass	1/2 teaspoon turmeric
3 kaffir lime leaves or bay leaves	pinch cayenne
2 half-ripe mangoes	1–2 teaspoons sugar
3 shallots	salt to taste
2 cloves garlic (optional)	1/2 cup water
1 1/2-inch piece ginger	

METHOD

■ Rub the fish with salt and lime juice inside and out and place the lemongrass and kaffir lime leaves or bay leaves inside the fish.

■ To make the sauce, peel the mangoes, cut two good slices from each, and cut these into julienne strips. Set aside. With a sharp knife, cut all the remaining flesh off the stones, purée in a blender, and set aside. Put the shallots, garlic, if desired, ginger, candlenuts or macadamia nuts, vinegar, and 1 tablespoon of the olive oil into the blender and blend to a smooth paste.

■ Heat the remaining oil in a wok or frying pan and fry the puréed shallot mixture, stirring continuously, for 2 minutes. Add the turmeric and cayenne, stir, then add the mango purée, sugar, and salt. Add the water and simmer gently for 5 minutes. Take the sauce off the stove, and set it aside to be reheated just before serving.

■ Steam the fish for about 15–20 minutes and arrange it on a serving dish. Reheat the sauce, add the julienne of mangoes, stir, and simmer for 2 minutes. Pour the hot mango sauce over the fish and serve immediately. In Indonesia, rice and vegetables would be the natural accompaniments, but this fish is equally good with pasta or new potatoes and salad.

Fish with Green Chile in Curry Sauce

KARE IKAN DENGAN LOMBOK HIJAU

SERVES 4–6

Goreng kakap, or fried sea perch, is a favorite dish with my family back home, but I have always preferred curried kakap with green chiles.

INGREDIENTS

2 pounds any white fish, filleted, cut into 1-inch squares	1 cup thick coconut milk, divided
1 teaspoon salt	4 large green chiles, seeded and cut diagonally
5 shallots or 1 onion, chopped	pinch galingal
3 cloves garlic, chopped	1 teaspoon ground coriander
1 1/2-inch piece ginger, chopped	1 teaspoon ground cumin
2 candlenuts or raw macadamia nuts (optional)	1/2 teaspoon turmeric
2 tablespoons olive oil	2 tablespoons tamarind water or 2 tamarind slices
2 tablespoons water	2 kaffir lime leaves or bay leaves

METHOD

■ Sprinkle the fish with salt.

■ To make the paste, put the shallots or onion, garlic, ginger, and candlenuts or macadamia nuts, if desired, into a blender with the oil and water, and blend until smooth.

■ In a saucepan heat 3 tablespoons of the coconut milk. Bring to a boil, stir for 1 minute, and add the paste from the blender. Continue stirring, add the chiles, galingal, coriander, cumin, turmeric, tamarind water or slices, and kaffir lime leaves or bay leaves. Then add the rest of the coconut milk. Let this bubble gently for 20–30 minutes, stirring often, until reduced by half.

■ Carefully put in the fish and continue cooking for 10 minutes. Taste, and adjust the seasoning. Serve hot with rice, accompanied by prawn crackers and lots of vegetables or salad.

51

Tuna Fish Saté

SATÉ AMBU-AMBU

SERVES 4 AS A STARTER, OR 6–8, EATEN WITH OTHER DISHES AND RICE

I had been trying for years to remember the name of a fish that my grandmother used to cook in Padang Panjang. On my last visit to Indonesia, the same fish appeared on my sister's table. I suggested that it was called *ambu-ambu*; she said *tongkol*. In a reference book I found that *tongkol* and *ambu-ambu* are alternative names for tuna.

INGREDIENTS

1 1/2 pounds fresh tuna fish, minced or cubed	Saté Lilit/ Minced Pork Saté Balinese-style marinade (page 32)

METHOD

■ If the fish is cubed, marinate it and put it on sticks as for Saté Bebek/Duck Saté Balinese-style (page 34). If it is minced, mix it with the marinade with your hand, kneading it for a while so that it becomes somewhat sticky. Then put it on sticks as for Saté Lilit (page 32).

■ Grill for 6 minutes, turning several times, or cook in the oven at 350°F for about 15 minutes. Serve hot, without sauce or with Nam Chim/Sweet and Sour Chile Sauce (page 145).

Sumatran Steamed Fish with Spices and Herbs

PANGEK BUNGKUS

This is best made with freshwater fish but is also tasty with saltwater fish. In Indonesia, the fish would be wrapped in banana leaves and cooked over charcoal or a wood fire. I cook mine in the oven wrapped with aluminum foil.

SERVES 10–12, WITH SEVERAL OTHER DISHES, FOR A BUFFET

INGREDIENTS

1 4- to 5-pound fish, gutted and scaled	3 candlenuts or raw macadamia nuts (optional)
2 tablespoons tamarind water or juice of 1 lime or lemon	2–4 large red chiles, seeded and chopped
1 teaspoon salt	1 cup very thick coconut milk, divided
1/2 teaspoon cayenne	1 teaspoon ground coriander
1 stalk lemongrass	pinch galingal
2 kaffir lime leaves or bay leaves	1/4 teaspoon turmeric
4 shallots	salt to taste
2 cloves garlic	2 tablespoons chopped mint or basil
	6 scallions, thinly sliced

METHOD

■ Make 2 diagonal slashes on each side of the fish, then rub the fish inside and out with tamarind water or lime or lemon juice, salt, and cayenne. Put the lemongrass and kaffir lime leaves or bay leaves inside the fish. Leave the fish in a cool place while preparing the rest of the ingredients.

■ To make the paste, put the shallots, garlic, candlenuts or macadamia nuts, if desired, and chiles in a blender with 4 tablespoons of the coconut milk, and blend to a smooth paste. Put the paste in a saucepan, bring to a boil, stir, and add the coriander, galingal, turmeric, and salt. Pour in the rest of the coconut milk and simmer until reduced by half. Adjust the seasoning and let cool.

■ Lay the fish on 3 layers of wide aluminum foil. Pour half the thick spiced mixture over it and a small amount inside the cavity. Turn the fish over and pour the rest of the mixture over it. Then spread the mint or basil and scallions all over the fish. Wrap the aluminum foil around the fish and steam it in the oven at 350°F for 35–40 minutes. Serve hot or cold.

Fried Fish with Candlenut Sauce

IKAN GORENG DENGAN SAMBAL KEMIRI

SERVES 4

When my family lived in West Java, a few miles outside Cirebon, during the Japanese occupation, we stayed for about a year at my mother's parents' house in a small village called Beran. My grandmother's house was big in an idyllic setting. Beyond the big front garden was a small river separating the garden and the main road: a good river for fishing. In the back garden, underneath several mango and guava trees, we had a pond full of ikan emas, or red carp, and mujair, a little fish that did not grow bigger than the palm of a small adult hand. We had these fish fried quite often, and my mother would make what we all called sambal muncang to go with the fried fish and rice. We ate with our hands, of course, breaking the crisp fish and dipping it in the sambal. Muncang is the local name for kemiri or candlenuts. Here I use red carp or red snapper, and I don't claim that my sambal kemiri is a copy of my mother's.

INGREDIENTS

4 whole red snapper, cleaned and gutted	1 teaspoon fried shrimp paste (optional)
2 teaspoons salt	1 teaspoon salt
2 tablespoons tamarind water or lemon juice	1 teaspoon sugar
pinch turmeric	1/2 cup thick coconut milk
5 candlenuts or raw macadamia nuts	2 tablespoons tamarind water
5 shallots, chopped	1 lime, cut into about 10 small pieces
2 cloves garlic, chopped	vegetable oil for deep-frying
3 red chiles, seeded and chopped, or 1 teaspoon Sambal Ulek/Crushed Red Chiles with Salt (page 139)	2 tablespoons rice flour or all-purpose flour

METHOD

■ Make 2 deep slashes on both sides of each fish and rub them well, inside and out, with the mixture of salt, tamarind water or lemon juice, and turmeric. Leave in a cool place for at least 30 minutes while preparing the sauce.

METHOD

■ To make the sauce, put all the remaining ingredients except the lime pieces, oil, and flour into a blender, and blend until smooth. Pour the mixture into a small saucepan, bring to a boil, and simmer, uncovered, for 12–15 minutes. Taste, and add more sugar or salt, if necessary, and the pieces of lime. Stir, and transfer to a bowl. Set aside.

■ Heat the oil in a wok or deep-fryer. Sprinkle the flour evenly over the fish. Fry 2 fish at a time, turning them over several times, until they are golden brown or the skin is slightly crisp. Serve hot or warm with the sauce.

Thai Grilled Caramelized Fish

PLA WAN

SERVES 4

I suggest you make this dish in the summer, outdoors on the barbecue. The fish is sprinkled generously with sugar before being grilled. The taste is superb but it can be quite messy if you do this under the broiler in the kitchen. I watched this being cooked in a restaurant in Bangkok; when the fish is smoking and quite charred it is served to you piping hot, and you eat it with your fingers. Usually a whole fish is used. Almost any fish can be cooked this way—small whole ones, or fillets or steaks of larger ones.

INGREDIENTS

4 sole	juice of 1 lime
1 teaspoon salt	4–6 tablespoons turbinado sugar

METHOD

■ Rub the fish with salt and lime juice and leave in a cool place until they are to be grilled. Just before grilling, rub the fish all over with the sugar and grill for 3 minutes each side, turning over once. Serve immediately, with a chile dip (Nam Chim/Sweet and Sour Chile Sauce, page 145) if you like it hot.

MEAT AND POULTRY

▲▲▲▲▲▲▲▲▲▲▲▲▲▲▲▲▲▲

Meat in tropical countries tends to be leaner and tougher than meat grown in temperate lands where the grass is lusher. This doesn't mean it has less flavor. In fact, it may have more: chickens, certainly, taste more like chickens when they have lived dangerously and ranged freely along the side of a main road. If you visit that part of the world, you may find that meat is cut up in unfamiliar ways. Even the animals are not quite the same: beef usually comes from buffaloes, and "lamb" usually means goat. However, none of these considerations is any obstacle to cooking good Thai and Indonesian meat dishes in the West.

Cooking time for some dishes is very short, one reason why the meat sometimes has to be cut up small; this takes time, but the result will justify it. Some recipes, on the other hand, such as Rendang (page 65) demand a very long cooking time, partly perhaps to make tough meat tender but, more important, because meat is expensive. We don't as a rule eat large quantities of meat at a sitting, nor do we eat meat by itself; we always have plenty of vegetables and rice with it.

Cooking in bamboo tubes

Madurese Lamb Curry

GULAI PARSANGA

SERVES 6–8

This curry should really be made with goat meat, but in countries where goats aren't eaten much, lamb is a good substitute. Like goat, it needs to be simmered a long time.

INGREDIENTS

1 cup freshly grated coconut or dried coconut	1 teaspoon turmeric
thin slice shrimp paste, about 1 inch square	2 pounds lamb, cut into bite-size pieces
2 tablespoons vegetable oil	1 stalk lemongrass or 1/2 teaspoon lemongrass powder
6 shallots or 2 onions, chopped	1 1-inch cinnamon stick
4 cloves garlic, chopped	6 cloves
1 teaspoon white pepper	1 1-inch piece ginger, chopped
2 teaspoons ground coriander	salt to taste
1 teaspoon ground cumin	1 cup hot water
1/2 teaspoon ground nutmeg	2 cups thick coconut milk
1/4 teaspoon galingal	

METHOD

▪ In a wok or frying pan, roast the grated or dried coconut, stirring continuously, until golden brown. Then grind finely, either in a grinder or with a pestle and mortar. Crush the shrimp paste on a plate with the back of a spoon.

▪ Heat the oil in a saucepan and fry the shallots or onions and garlic for 1–2 minutes, then add the pepper, coriander, cumin, nutmeg, galingal, and turmeric. Stir, and add the lamb. Stir again, cover, and simmer for 2 minutes. Uncover, and stir in the coconut, lemongrass, cinnamon, cloves, ginger, shrimp paste, and salt.

▪ Add the hot water and simmer for 20 minutes. Add the coconut milk and continue to simmer for 20–30 minutes, stirring occasionally, or until the sauce is thick and the lamb tender. Remove the cinnamon and lemongrass. Serve hot with rice.

Lamb in Black Bean Sauce

KAMBING MASAK TAUCO

SERVES 4–6

Most Indonesians prefer yellow bean sauce to black. Both have the same name, "tauco." Yellow tauco is used mostly with chicken or vegetables, when you want plenty of sauce; for a "dry-fried" dish black tauco is better, as the Chinese know. In a Chinese restaurant you would expect this dish to be made with pork. People of my parents' generation, if they are strict Moslems, will not eat in Chinese restaurants, but younger people do, simply asking whether a dish has pork in it. The combination of black beans with green chiles is just right in this dish. Note that the meat can be marinated well in advance if desired.

INGREDIENTS

1 1/2 pounds lean meat from a leg of lamb, thinly sliced	5 shallots, thinly sliced
1 tablespoon light soy sauce	4 cloves garlic, chopped
1 teaspoon mild vinegar	1 1/2-inch piece ginger, chopped
4 tablespoons black tauco (black bean sauce)	4 green chiles, seeded and sliced diagonally
1/2 cup peanut oil	1 tablespoon dark soy sauce, preferably Indonesian kecap manis

METHOD

■ Rub the lamb with the light soy sauce and vinegar. Put it in a bowl and let it marinate for 1 hour or more in the refrigerator.

■ To make the sauce, soak the black tauco in cold water for 10 minutes, then drain and rinse. Mash them, not too smoothly, on a plate with the back of a spoon.

■ Heat the oil in a wok or frying pan, and fry the lamb in batches for 3 minutes each time. Take it out with a slotted spoon and drain on paper towels. Retain about 2 tablespoons of the oil and discard the rest. Fry the shallots, garlic, and ginger, stirring continuously for 2 minutes. Add the green chiles, the mashed black tauco, and dark soy sauce; continue stir-frying for 1 minute, then add the lamb. Stir continuously again for 2 minutes. Serve hot with boiled rice.

Hot and Sour Lamb

KAMBING ASAM PEDAS

SERVES 4–6

Most Indonesian dishes with hot and sour sauce come from West Sumatra, where I was born. My grandmother would always cook this with tamarind and lots of red chiles crushed into a smooth paste. The sauce was very red, really hot and sour, and delicious.

The recipe that follows will look and taste just as good but will not be burning hot. If tamarind is not available, use mild vinegar.

INGREDIENTS

1 1/2 pounds lean meat from a leg of lamb, cut in bite-size pieces	1 teaspoon ground coriander
1 teaspoon salt	1 6-ounce can bamboo shoots
4 shallots	1 green or yellow bell pepper, seeded
2 cloves garlic	1/2 cup vegetable oil
1 1/2-inch piece ginger	3 tablespoons tamarind water or 2 tamarind slices or 2 tablespoons mild vinegar
2 large red chiles, seeded, or 1/2 teaspoon cayenne	1/2 cup cold water
4 candlenuts or raw macadamia nuts or 1/2 cup thick coconut milk	salt to taste

METHOD

▪ Put the lamb in a bowl, and rub it well with the salt. Set it aside in a cool place for about 10 minutes.

▪ Put the shallots, garlic, ginger, red chiles, candlenuts or macadamia nuts or coconut milk into a blender and blend until smooth. If you are using candlenuts or macadamia nuts, add 4 tablespoons water to the mixture. Add the coriander.

▪ Cut the bamboo shoots and pepper into diamond-shaped slices. Blanch the pepper.

▪ In a wok or large saucepan, heat the oil and fry the meat in batches for 3 minutes each time. Take it out with a slotted spoon and drain on paper towels. Discard the remaining oil, except for about 2 tablespoons. Fry the shallot paste, stirring continuously, for 3 minutes. Add the tamarind water or tamarind slices or vinegar, bamboo shoots, and water, and simmer for 3 minutes. Add the lamb and continue stirring for 2 minutes. Then add the pepper and stir for 1 minute longer. Taste, and add salt, if necessary. If using tamarind slices, discard these before serving. Serve hot with rice or pasta.

Beef Curry with Peanuts

MUSAMAN CURRY

SERVES 4–6

The sauce of this curry needs to be dark brown and very thick. It is customary to add small cubes of fresh ripe pineapple and the peanuts a minute before you are finished boiling the sauce.

INGREDIENTS

5 shallots	2–3 cloves
2 cloves garlic	1 tablespoon crumbled shrimp paste
1 1-inch stalk lemongrass, outer leaves discarded	2 tablespoons vegetable oil
2 tablespoons chopped cilantro	1 1/2 pounds beef brisket or steak, cut into 1-inch cubes
4 red chiles, seeded	3 tablespoons tamarind water or 2 tamarind slices
1 tablespoon coriander	1 tablespoon turbinado sugar
1 teaspoon cumin	2 kaffir lime leaves or bay leaves
2 cardamom seeds	3 cups thick coconut milk
2 tablespoons oil	salt to taste
2 tablespoons water	1 small pineapple, cut into small cubes (optional)
1/2 teaspoon galingal	1/4 pound roasted peanuts, chopped
1/2 teaspoon ground nutmeg	
1/2 teaspoon ground cinnamon	

METHOD

■ To make the paste, put the shallots, garlic, lemongrass, cilantro, chiles, coriander, cumin, and cardamom on a baking tray and roast in the oven at 350°F for 10 minutes. Or you can put them in a heavy skillet or frying pan and brown on the stove, shaking the pan frequently. Transfer to a blender, add the oil and water, and blend until smooth. Add the galingal, nutmeg, cinnamon, cloves, and shrimp paste.

■ In a large saucepan, heat the oil and fry the curry paste, stirring continuously with a wooden spoon, for 3 minutes. Add the beef, stir until all the pieces are coated with the paste, then add the tamarind water or tamarind slices. Cover and simmer for 3 minutes. Uncover, and add the sugar, kaffir lime leaves or bay leaves, and coconut milk.

■ Simmer uncovered for about 1 1/2 hours until the sauce becomes very thick. Stir frequently when the sauce starts to thicken. Taste, and add salt, if necessary. Add the pineapple, if desired, and peanuts. Stir for 1 more minute. Serve hot with boiled rice.

Red Curry of Beef

GAENG PED NEUA

SERVES 4–6

This Thai curry somewhat resembles the traditional Rendang from West Sumatra (page 65), but the taste is different, as this curry has many more spices in it.

INGREDIENTS

5 shallots or 1 onion	15 large dried red chiles, seeded, or 1 teaspoon cayenne
3 cloves garlic	1 stalk fresh lemongrass, chopped
1/2 teaspoon galingal	2 teaspoons crumbled shrimp paste
3 tablespoons chopped cilantro	1 teaspoon ground white pepper
5 strips dried kaffir lime peel	1 tablespoon salt
1 tablespoon roasted coriander	5 cups coconut milk, divided
1 teaspoon roasted cumin	2 1/2 pounds beef brisket or steak, cut into 3/4-inch cubes
1/2 teaspoon ground nutmeg	
1/2 teaspoon ground mace	

METHOD

■ Put all the ingredients except the beef and only 5 tablespoons of the coconut milk into a blender and blend to a smooth paste.

■ In a large saucepan, heat about 1/2 cup of the coconut milk. When it boils, add the paste, stir, and simmer until the coconut milk becomes oily. Continue stirring for another 2 minutes, then add the beef and stir again until all the pieces are coated with the paste. Add the rest of the coconut milk. Let the curry bubble gently for about 2 hours until the meat is tender and the sauce thick. Taste, and add salt, if necessary. Serve hot with boiled rice.

Note: This curry can be reheated in a saucepan or in a microwave oven. It can also be frozen successfully. Thaw it out completely before reheating.

Beef Fried with Green Peppers

NUA PUD PRIK

SERVES 4

This is a standard dish in Thai, Chinese, or Malaysian restaurants. The ingredients vary from one area to another. I often use leftovers from the Sunday roast beef. If you use leftover roast beef, the marinade and initial frying are not necessary.

INGREDIENTS

2 teaspoons corn flour or potato flour	about 1/2 cup peanut or sunflower oil
1 tablespoon light soy sauce	4 scallions, cut diagonally into strips
1/4 teaspoon cayenne	2 cloves garlic, crushed
1 1-inch piece ginger, minced	1/4 teaspoon cayenne
1 pound rump steak or leftover roast beef, cut across the grain into bite-size pieces	2 tablespoons light soy sauce
1–2 medium green bell peppers, seeded	1 tablespoon fish sauce
	1 teaspoon sugar
1/2 pound baby corn (optional)	1 teaspoon rice vinegar

METHOD

■ To make the marinade, mix the flour, soy sauce, cayenne, and ginger in a bowl. Add the pieces of beef, and mix again so that every piece is well coated. Leave in a cool place for at least 30 minutes.

■ Cut the peppers into strips about 3/4-inch wide, then cut each strip diagonally into 4 or 5 pieces. Cut each baby corn, if desired, diagonally also to about the same size as the peppers.

■ In a wok or frying pan, heat the oil. Fry the peppers in batches for 2 minutes each time. Take the peppers out with a slotted spoon and drain on paper towels. Do the same with the baby corn. Strain the oil back into the wok or frying pan to get rid of any fragments of baby corn.

■ Reheat the oil and fry the beef in batches, stirring continuously, for 2 minutes each time. Remove with a slotted spoon. By the time you finish frying the beef, there will be just enough oil left to go on to the next step. If there still seems to be too much, discard some, leaving only about 2 tablespoons.

■ Reheat the oil again, add the scallions, garlic, and cayenne, stir, and add the soy sauce, fish sauce, and sugar. Stir again, and add the beef, peppers, and baby corn. Continue stirring and turning for 1–2 minutes. Taste, and add salt, if necessary. Serve immediately with rice or noodles.

A Traditional West Sumatran Dish

RENDANG

SERVES 10–12

Rendang is nothing like a curry. A well-cooked one is brown, sometimes almost black. It should be chunky and dry, yet succulent, with the dryness of meat that has absorbed its juices and its sauce during a long period of cooking. The cooking process is, I think, unique, for it is the only dish I know of that passes from boiling to frying without any interruption. The cooking time is therefore very long.

There are several different basic ingredients you can use as the foundation of the dish. For instance there is a "Rendang Nangka" (Jackfruit Rendang), a lovely vegetarian dish. The traditional Rendang, as I learned it from my grandmother in Padang Panjang, West Sumatra, used buffalo meat, and it was almost always cooked in large quantities.

INGREDIENTS

6 shallots, thinly sliced	1/2 teaspoon galingal
4 cloves garlic	1 salam leaf or bay leaf
1 1-inch piece ginger, chopped	1 stalk fresh lemongrass, bruised
6 red chiles, seeded and chopped, or 3 teaspoons cayenne	2 teaspoons salt
6 cups coconut milk	3 pounds beef brisket or rump steak, cut into large cubes
1 teaspoon turmeric	

METHOD

■ Put the shallots, garlic, ginger, and chiles in a blender or a food processor and reduce to a purée. Place the purée and coconut milk in a large wok with the turmeric and galingal. Add the salam leaf or bay leaf, lemongrass, salt, and beef, which must be completely covered by the coconut milk. Stir, and start cooking on medium heat, uncovered. Let this simmer for 2 hours, stirring occasionally. By this time the coconut milk should be quite thick and oily; it needs to be stirred frequently. Taste, and add more salt, if necessary.

■ When it becomes thick and brown, stir continuously for about 15 minutes. The dish is ready when the oil has been almost completely absorbed by the meat. Serve hot with plenty of rice.

Note: Rendang will keep for more than 1 week in the refrigerator. It can be reheated as often as you like. It can be frozen successfully for 5–6 months. Thaw it completely before you heat it in a baking dish in a moderate oven for 10–15 minutes.

Beef Stew with Potatoes

GULAI DAGING DENGAN KENTANG

SERVES 6–8

In Indonesia we used to make this in the time of the Japanese occupation, when food, especially meat, was scarce and very expensive. Any vegetables that we could dig up or pick from the garden went into the stew, not just potatoes. But when good ingredients are available this will make an excellent but still economical dish for a large party or a family gathering, adding one other vegetable. Here I suggest spaghetti squash or pumpkin. Serve the stew with garlic bread, pasta or rice, and salad, or just salad.

INGREDIENTS

1 tablespoon rice flour or all-purpose flour	4 cloves garlic, minced
1 teaspoon salt	2 teaspoons ground coriander
1 tablespoon tamarind water or 1 teaspoon vinegar	1/2 teaspoon cayenne
	1/2 teaspoon turmeric
2 pounds beef brisket or rump steak, cut into 1/2-inch cubes	1/2 teaspoon ground ginger
2 pounds small new potatoes or large potatoes, cubed	2 kaffir lime leaves or bay leaves
	3 cups thick coconut milk, divided
1/2 cup vegetable oil	salt to taste
6 shallots or 2 onions, minced	2 pounds spaghetti squash or pumpkin, peeled and cubed

METHOD

■ To make the marinade, mix the flour, salt, and tamarind water or vinegar. Add the beef and rub each piece well with the marinade. Set aside.

■ Keep the prepared potatoes in a bowl of salted water.

■ In a large saucepan, heat the oil and fry the beef in 3 or 4 batches for 3 minutes each time, stirring continuously. Remove with a slotted spoon.

■ Keep about 2 tablespoons of the oil and discard the rest. Fry the shallots or onions and garlic, stirring continuously, for 2 minutes. Add the coriander, cayenne, turmeric, and ginger, stir, and add the kaffir lime leaves or bay leaves, half the coconut milk, and salt. Stir, bring to a boil, and add the beef. Simmer gently for 40 minutes. By the end of this time the meat should be almost tender and the sauce should be getting thick.

■ Add the rest of the coconut milk, and continue cooking for 10 minutes. Add the potato, cook for another 10 minutes, then add the squash or pumpkin and cook for 10 more minutes, or until the potatoes and squash or pumpkin are cooked. The sauce should not be too thick. Serve hot.

Note: This gulai can be reheated. It is good served on a buffet.

Beef Saté

SATÉ DAGING

SERVES 4

This is, I suppose, the classic Indonesian dish that everyone knows. It came originally from the Middle East and is closely related to shish kebab, which it obviously has a lot in common with. As long as you use a tender meat (rump steak is my favorite) you can hardly go wrong.

INGREDIENTS

3 shallots, thinly sliced	2 tablespoons light soy sauce
2 cloves garlic, chopped (optional)	2 tablespoons peanut or olive oil
1 tablespoon white malt vinegar	1 pound rump steak, cut into 3/4-inch cubes
2 teaspoons ground coriander	
1/2–1 teaspoon cayenne	8–12 10-inch wooden saté sticks or metal skewers
1/2 teaspoon salt	

METHOD

■ To make the marinade, mix the shallots, garlic, if desired, vinegar, coriander, cayenne, salt, soy sauce, and oil in a bowl. Add the beef and stir well to make sure every piece is covered. Let stand for at least 2 hours or overnight in the refrigerator.

■ Discard the marinade and put the meat on the skewers. Broil, turning several times, for 6–8 minutes. Grilling on charcoal will give an even better flavor.

■ Eat hot, with saté sauce or sambal kecap. In Indonesia, we usually also sprinkle fried shallots or crisp fried onions over the saté just before serving.

Dry-Fried (or Grilled) Beef

DENDENG DAGING

SERVES 4–6

As with saté, the flavor of Dendeng depends very much on the marinade. Of course it also depends on the meat; you need a tender cut, as the cooking time is very short.

The traditional Dendeng Daging is sweet. After being marinated the beef is dried in the tropical sun and then deep-fried until crisp. It should be tender and brittle, but if the drying is not just right it can become leathery and tough. In this recipe, however, you will not need to worry about whether the day is sunny or not, because there is no need to dry the meat. I like a good garlicky marinade, but use less garlic if you prefer.

INGREDIENTS

8 cloves garlic	1 1/2-inch cinnamon stick
2 shallots	1 teaspoon salt
1 teaspoon black peppercorns	1 tablespoon dark soy sauce or kecap manis
1 tablespoon coriander	
2 candlenuts or raw macadamia nuts or 5 tablespoons thick coconut cream	2 tablespoons sunflower or olive oil
	1 1/2 pounds rump steak, thinly sliced
2 tablespoons tamarind water or 2 teaspoons vinegar	2 tablespoons grated palm sugar or brown sugar (optional)
1/2 teaspoon ground nutmeg	

METHOD

■ To make the marinade, put the garlic, shallots, peppercorns, coriander, candlenuts or macadamia nuts or coconut cream, tamarind water or vinegar, nutmeg, cinnamon, salt, soy sauce or kecap manis, and oil in a blender and blend into a smooth paste. Transfer to a bowl and add the slices of beef with the paste, mixing them thoroughly so that they are well coated. Marinate for at least 2 hours or overnight in the refrigerator. If you like your dendeng rather sweet, coat the slices with the sugar before cooking.

■ Grill or shallow-fry the meat in a nonstick frying pan for not more than 3 minutes total, turning the slices over once. Serve immediately. My choice with dendeng is fried rice (page 89), with a salad or green vegetables.

Sweet Pork with Marigold

MOO WAN

SERVES 4

My Thai friend Noot (Mrs. Kamolvan Punyashthiti) has given me a number of recipes for this book. Some I have adapted a little, but this one, I hope, is exactly as she would cook it herself. She told me that it looks particularly good if you sprinkle it with marigold petals, and that French marigolds are best. Use other flower petals instead, if you like—nasturtiums are quite nice—or leave the petals out altogether. But mix some shrimp paste with the pork at the end of cooking. Serve the sweet pork on top of boiled fragrant Thai rice.

INGREDIENTS

1 tablespoon dark soy sauce	2 tablespoons fish sauce
1/4 teaspoon salt	1 tablespoon dark soy sauce
1 pound pork fillet, cut into small bite-size pieces	1/4 teaspoon salt
	1/4 teaspoon pepper
2 tablespoons peanut oil	8 tablespoons hot water
1 onion, minced	1 teaspoon fried shrimp paste
2 tablespoons grated palm sugar or turbinado sugar	2 tablespoons chopped cilantro
1/2 teaspoon ground white pepper	handful marigold petals

METHOD

▪ Rub the soy sauce and salt into the pork pieces. Set aside in a cool place.

▪ To make the sauce, heat the oil in a wok or frying pan, and fry the onion until soft. Add the sugar, pepper, and fish sauce, and stir vigorously with a wooden spoon until the sugar has caramelized.

▪ Add the pork, stir-fry for 3 minutes, then add the soy sauce, salt, pepper, and hot water, and continue cooking on high heat for 3 minutes, stirring frequently. Add the shrimp paste, and stir-fry again for a few seconds.

▪ Garnish with cilantro and marigold petals. Serve hot with rice.

Hot and Sour Pork

BABI ASAM PEDAS

SERVES 4

There are different versions of this dish all over Southeast Asia. Mine is one that I used during the three years I operated a delicatessen: I know it works well, and my customers liked it.

INGREDIENTS

1 teaspoon salt	2 large red chiles, seeded and chopped, or 1 1/2 teaspoons cayenne
2 teaspoons white malt vinegar	
1 pound lean pork fillet, cut into 3/4-inch cubes	1/2 cup sunflower or olive oil, divided
	6 tablespoons water, divided
4 shallots or 1 onion	3 tablespoons white malt vinegar
2 cloves garlic	1 tablespoon sugar
1 1-inch piece ginger	1 6-ounce can bamboo shoots, drained and rinsed
3 candlenuts or raw macadamia nuts (optional)	salt to taste
	3 tablespoons chopped mint or basil

METHOD

■ Rub the salt and vinegar into the pork pieces and leave for 30 minutes.

■ To make the sauce, put the shallots or onion, garlic, ginger, candlenuts or macadamia nuts, if desired, and chiles into a blender. Add 2 tablespoons of the oil and 2 tablespoons of the water, and blend into a smooth paste.

■ Heat the remaining oil in a wok or frying pan and fry the pieces of pork in batches for 4–5 minutes each time. Remove with a slotted spoon.

■ Discard the oil, except for about 2 tablespoons. Reheat this and fry the paste from the blender, stirring continuously for 3 minutes. Add the vinegar and sugar, stir, then add the remaining water, bamboo shoots, and pork. Simmer for 2 minutes. Taste, and add salt, if necessary. Stir again for another minute, add the mint or basil, and stir again. Serve immediately with rice or boiled new potatoes.

Note: This dish can be frozen satisfactorily. Thaw it completely before reheating in a saucepan, stirring occasionally, until hot.

Stuffed Chiles in Nets

PRIK YUAK SOD SAI

SERVES 6–8

For this dish, choose the largest green chiles you can find. They should be light green or yellowish in color, not dark—the dark ones are much hotter.

INGREDIENTS

12–16 large mild green chiles	1 tablespoon fish sauce
1/2 pound ground pork	1 teaspoon salt
1/4 pound raw prawns or shrimps, peeled and minced	1 teaspoon sugar
2 tablespoons chopped cilantro	5 eggs, divided
2 cloves garlic, chopped	large pinch salt
2 tablespoons chopped scallions	1 tablespoon olive oil
6 water chestnuts, chopped	
1 tablespoon light soy sauce	

METHOD

- Cut the tops off the chiles and scoop out the seeds.

- To make the stuffing, in a bowl mix the pork and prawns thoroughly with a fork. Add the cilantro, garlic, scallions, and water chestnuts and continue mixing, either with a fork or by hand. Add the soy sauce and fish sauce, and season with salt and sugar. Finally add the egg and mix everything thoroughly. Divide this mixture into 12 or 16 portions and stuff the chiles with it. Steam them for 12–15 minutes.

- To make the nets, break the eggs into another bowl and add the salt. Flick your fingers of one hand lightly through the eggs once or twice to break up the yolks and distribute the salt without totally mixing yolks and whites.

- Rub a nonstick frying pan with oil and heat it until it is just warm. Dip your fingers of one hand into the egg and move your hand from side to side, forward and back above the frying pan, letting the liquid egg run from your fingertips to form a network of lines. Leave the egg-net for about a minute, then lift it carefully onto a flat plate.

- Continue making nets until all the egg is used up. Roll and wrap the stuffed chiles in the nets. Serve warm or cold as a snack with drinks or as an accompaniment to a rice meal.

Slices of Pork Fried with Ginger and Mushrooms

MUH PUD PRIK

SERVES 4

If you have had this dish in a restaurant you probably noticed that the sauce was thickened with corn flour immediately before serving. This produces a gooey sauce which I find unappetizing. If you follow my method, using the flour to marinate the meat, the sauce will appear thickened but not sticky, and it will taste much better.

INGREDIENTS

1 tablespoon light soy sauce	1 1-inch piece ginger, chopped
1 tablespoon corn flour or all-purpose flour	1/2 cup hot water
pinch cayenne	1 tablespoon dark soy sauce
1 tablespoon rice vinegar	1 tablespoon fish sauce
1 pound pork fillet, thinly sliced	salt and pepper to taste
5 tablespoons vegetable oil	1 tablespoon chopped cilantro
1/2 pound button mushrooms, halved	2 tablespoons chopped scallions
2 cloves garlic, crushed	

METHOD

■ To make the marinade, mix together the soy sauce, flour, cayenne, and vinegar in a bowl. Add the pork slices, and marinate for at least 2 hours in the refrigerator.

■ Heat the oil in a wok or frying pan. Fry the mushrooms for 2 minutes. Remove with a slotted spoon and drain on paper towels. Reheat the oil, add half of the pork, and stir-fry for 2 minutes. Remove the pork with a slotted spoon and transfer to a bowl. Repeat with the remaining pork.

■ You should have some clear oil in the wok or frying pan by now, with some flour from the marinade sticking to the bottom. This will thicken the sauce at the end of cooking. Discard most of the oil, leaving about 1 tablespoon.

■ Heat this oil, then add the garlic and ginger. Stir, then add the water, soy sauce, and fish sauce. Continue stirring. The sauce should be starting to thicken by now. Add the pork and mushrooms and season with salt and pepper. Stir-fry for 2 minutes.

■ Just before serving, add the cilantro and scallions and stir for 1/2 more minute. Serve immediately with boiled rice, noodles, or pasta.

Spicy Minced Pork Fried in Batter

TOD MAN MUH

SERVES 4–6

Some people spell this Tod Mun. There are several dishes with this name; this one is made with ground pork. Every country has its own kind of meatballs, with different kinds of meat. This Thai version is good and spicy. The meatballs or cakes are normally flattened a little, like Tod Man Pla Krai/Savory Fish Cake (page 125), before being deep-fried.

INGREDIENTS

1/4 cup rice flour or all-purpose flour	4 kaffir lime leaves or bay leaves
1/2 teaspoon salt	big handful string beans, sliced into thin rounds
1/2 teaspoon ground white pepper	
1/2 cup cold water	2 teaspoons sugar
2 teaspoons oive oil	1/2 teaspoon salt
1 1/2 pounds ground pork	2 teaspoons light soy sauce
5 shallots, chopped	1 tablespoon fish sauce
4 cloves garlic, chopped	2 tablespoons olive oil
4 red chiles, seeded and chopped	vegetable oil for deep-frying
4 tablespoons chopped cilantro	

METHOD

■ To make the batter, mix the flour, salt, pepper, water, and oil in a bowl, stirring vigorously with a wooden spoon. The batter should be quite thin.

■ In a separate bowl mix the minced pork with all the other ingredients except the oil used later for deep-frying. Let it marinate for 30–40 minutes, or overnight in the refrigerator.

■ Take about 1 tablespoon of the meat, put it on the palm of your hand, and form it into a ball. Use up all the meat in the same way. You can store the meatballs in the refrigerator or freezer; if you freeze them, thaw out completely before frying.

■ Flatten the meatballs between the palms of your hands, pressing them gently. Then dip them one by one in the batter. Fry them 5 or 6 at a time for 3–4 minutes in deep oil in a wok. Remove them with a slotted spoon and drain on paper towels. Serve them hot with boiled rice and a vegetable dish.

Note: The Tomato Sauce on page 144 is good to serve with this. You can garnish this dish with Goreng Bawang/Fried Shallots (page 141).

Green Curry of Chicken

GAENG KEO WAN KAI

SERVES 4–6

The sauce for this Thai curry can be very liquid and runny, or it can be reduced and made quite thick. Personally, I don't like the sauce too thick. The sauce is made from curry paste mixed with coconut milk; if you do not like coconut milk, substitute chicken stock and yogurt.

INGREDIENTS

4 shallots, chopped	1 green bell pepper (optional)
3 cloves garlic, chopped	2 tablespoons chopped cilantro
1/2 stalk lemongrass, outer leaves removed	1/2 teaspoon shrimp paste
1 tablespoon chopped cilantro	2 teaspoons salt
3/4-inch piece fresh galingal, chopped	2 tablespoons vegetable oil
1 teaspoon grated kaffir lime peel	1 2 1/2- to 3-pound chicken or 2 pounds chicken breast and thighs, boneless, cut into 3/4-inch cubes
1 teaspoon ground pepper	
1 tablespoon roasted coriander	
1 teaspoon roasted cumin	4 cups coconut milk or 3 cups chicken stock and 1 cup yogurt
1/2 teaspoon ground mace	
1/2 teaspoon ground nutmeg	1 pound new potatoes
5 fresh green chiles, seeded	

METHOD

■ To make the paste, blend together the shallots, garlic, lemongrass, cilantro, galingal, kaffir lime peel, pepper, coriander, cumin, mace, nutmeg, bell pepper, if desired, cilantro, shrimp paste, and salt in a food processor. Heat the oil in a saucepan and fry the paste, stirring continuously, for 2–3 minutes. Add the chicken pieces and stir until all the pieces are well coated with the paste. Reduce the heat, cover the pan, and let it simmer for 4 minutes.

■ If you are using coconut milk, stir it in and simmer, stirring frequently, for 50 minutes. Add the potatoes, and continue cooking for 10–15 minutes, or until the potatoes are cooked. Serve hot with boiled rice.

■ If you are using stock and yogurt, add the stock (use the chicken bones to make it) instead of the coconut milk. Simmer for 50 minutes, then remove the pan from the heat for 10 minutes. Stir in the yogurt, and bring the mixture slowly back to a gentle boil (to prevent curdling). Add the potatoes, and stir frequently until cooked (as above).

Stuffed Chicken Wings

PEEK KAI YOD SAI

SERVES 4-6

This is a dish you will find often in Thailand and in Indonesia, and indeed in several other Southeast Asian countries. Maybe it was a Chinese dish originally; I remember eating it often in a Chinese restaurant when I lived in Yogyakarta. The Chinese and the Thais use pork as one of the ingredients for the stuffing, and what follows is the Thai version of the recipe. By omitting the pork and cilantro, you will make it an Indonesian dish.

INGREDIENTS

12 chicken wings	1 tablespoon light soy sauce
1/4 pound ground pork	1 teaspoon sugar
1/4 pound peeled raw shrimps, minced	1 teaspoon salt
4 scallions, thinly sliced	1 egg
4 tablespoons chopped cilantro	3 tablespoons rice flour or fine fresh breadcrumbs
1 red or green chile, seeded and chopped, or 1/4 teaspoon cayenne	vegetable oil for deep-frying
2 cloves garlic, chopped	

METHOD

■ Using a sharp knife, slit the skin of each chicken wing from the wing-tip joint along the length of the wing. Carefully separate the bones at the joints, then remove the bones and the meat from the skin. Try to leave the bony wing-tip in place, attached to the skin; it makes a good handle if you eat with your fingers. However, this is not really important.

■ To make the stuffing, mix the ground pork with the remaining ingredients except the egg, rice flour or breadcrumbs, and oil. Beat the egg and spread the flour or breadcrumbs on a flat plate.

■ Divide the stuffing into 12 portions and roll each portion in the skin of a chicken wing. When all 12 are done, dip them one at a time in the beaten egg and roll them over in the rice flour or breadcrumbs.

■ Steam the stuffed wings for 4 minutes. Let them cool before deep-frying, a few at a time, until golden brown. Serve whole as snacks, or slice them like sausages and serve with salad. These slices are also good for mixing with stir-fried vegetables or fried noodles.

Note: These stuffed wings can be frozen after steaming, and then fried straight from the freezer.

Grilled Chicken, Menado-Style

AYAM RICA-RICA

SERVES 4

Rica-rica (pronounced *reetja-reetja*) is usually very hot. A friend of mine who gave me this recipe said she used up to 20 large red chiles for one chicken. The idea is that the whole chicken should be covered in the red chile paste. To make the same quantity of paste with fewer chiles, I use more shallots and, like the Menadonese, I also put in some tomatoes; but since there are many areas of Indonesia where tomatoes aren't used, I have shown these as optional. I wrap the chicken in aluminum foil to preserve the sauce in the early stages of cooking.

INGREDIENTS

2 2 1/2-pound chickens	1 2-inch piece ginger
1 teaspoon salt	1 1/2-inch slice shrimp paste (optional)
juice of 1 lime	2 tablespoons oil
2 tablespoons oil or melted butter	2 tablespoons water
10 shallots or 2 onions	4 tomatoes, peeled, seeded, and chopped (optional)
4 cloves garlic	
4 red chiles, seeded	1/2 tablespoon salt

METHOD

■ Split the chickens lengthwise into halves and trim off some of the skin, fat, and bones. Rub the four halves with salt, lime juice, and oil or butter. Leave in a cool place while you prepare the other ingredients.

■ To make the spice paste, put the shallots or onions, garlic, chiles, ginger, and shrimp paste, if desired, into a blender with the oil and water. Blend until smooth. Pour this paste into a saucepan, bring to a boil, and stir continuously for 4 minutes. Add the tomatoes, if desired, and continue cooking and stirring for 1 minute. Taste, and add salt, if necessary. Remove from the stove and let col.

■ When the paste is cool, use half of it to rub over the chickens, rubbing under the skin as well. Then put each half-chicken on aluminum foil. Put the remaining paste on top of each half-chicken. Wrap the halves in the foil, sealing at the top of each parcel.

■ Cook in the oven at 325°F for 45 minutes. Then open up the foil wrapping and broil for 4–6 minutes. Slide the chickens and the sauce onto a serving dish and serve at once.

Aromatic Chicken

AYAM DIBULUH

SERVES 4–6

Ayam dibuluh literally means chicken in bamboo. All Southeast Asian countries have many kinds of bamboo of different sizes, which are put to many uses. One of the most obvious is as cooking vessels—cheap and disposable. Outdoor cooking, on charcoal or wood fires, is also very natural in the tropics, so all these countries have lots of recipes for food cooked in bamboo.

This chicken dish is from Menado in North Sulawesi. My version, like that of the Balinese Ayam Betutu (page 78), is baked in rolls of aluminum foil in the oven or on a grill. The raw materials can be prepared a day in advance. If you can't find all the herbs, try using herbs from your own garden and substitute black or green pepper for the chiles.

INGREDIENTS

1 3- to 3 1/2-pound chicken with giblets or 2 1/4 pounds chicken meat (from breast and thighs) plus 4 chicken livers	1/2 stalk lemongrass, outer leaves discarded, minced
2 tablespoons lemon or lime juice	1 pandanus leaf, minced
1/2 teaspoon salt	4 kaffir lime leaves or bay leaves, minced
4 shallots, thinly sliced	4 scallions, thinly sliced
2 large green chiles, seeded and minced	2 tablespoons chopped mint
1 1-inch piece ginger, minced	2 tablespoons chopped basil
3 cloves garlic, minced	2 green tomatoes, minced
	2 tablespoons olive oil

METHOD

■ Skin, bone, and chop the chicken and the livers. Mix the chicken with the lemon or lime juice and salt in a bowl.

■ In a frying pan, fry the shallots, chiles, ginger, garlic, lemongrass, pandanus leaf, kaffir lime leaves or bay leaves, scallions, mint, basil, and tomatoes in the oil, stirring continuously, for 2–3 minutes. Allow to cool. Then add the chopped chicken and liver, kneading for several minutes.

■ Form the mixture into a large sausage and wrap with several layers of aluminum foil, rolling it several times until you have a firmly stuffed "sausage" about 10 inches long.

■ Preheat the oven to 350°F and cook for 1 hour to 1 hour 10 minutes. Serve hot or cold in thick slices. This can be stored in the refrigerator overnight, or in a freezer for up to 3 months. If you freeze it, make sure it is totally thawed out before cooking.

Balinese Chicken

AYAM BETUTU

SERVES 4

This, made with duck, is a traditional Balinese dish; the monks of Ubud still cook it in the old-fashioned way, leaving it for six or seven hours in the embers of a fire laid in a shallow trench. The duck is stuffed and wrapped in *seludang mayang,* the flower-sheath of a particular kind of palm, then layers and layers of banana leaves. An excellent alternative is to use aluminum foil, as described here; but remember that you need plenty—the chicken must be wrapped in several layers. I watched a Balinese friend cook a young chicken, using the same recipe but in an electric oven; it tasted extremely good. This is really her recipe, except that instead of the whole chicken I suggest using just the thighs and breast, boned but with the skin still on.

I use kale for the stuffing in autumn and winter; in spring and summer, I use spinach. Whatever green you use, you need to blanch it first, squeeze out excess water, and shred it finely.

Don't be put off by the long list of spices. The result is well worth the trouble.

INGREDIENTS

5 shallots	1/2 teaspoon white pepper
4 cloves garlic	1 2-inch piece lemongrass or 1/2 teaspoon lemongrass powder
5 red chiles, seeded, or 1 teaspoon cayenne	1 2-inch slice shrimp paste
5 tablespoons very thick coconut milk	juice of 1 lime
3 teaspoons coriander	2 tablespoons vegetable oil
2 teaspoons cumin	2 tablespoons water
2 cloves	2 tablespoons oil
1 2-inch cinnamon stick	2 teaspoons salt, divided
1/2 teaspoon ground nutmeg	1/4 pound kale
1/2 teaspoon turmeric	4 chicken breasts or 8 chicken thighs, boned but not skinned
1/2 teaspoon galingal	

METHOD

■ To make the spice mixture, blend the first 17 ingredients in a food processor. Or you can use a pestle and mortar if you prefer. In a frying pan, fry this paste in the oil, stirring continuously, for about 5 minutes, or until the smell of raw shallots and garlic has been replaced by a pleasant spicy fragrance. Add half the salt, and let cool.

METHOD

■ Mix half of the cooled paste in a bowl with the kale. Then rub the remaining salt evenly into the chicken pieces. Rub the spices into every part of the chicken, including under the skin. Stuff the kale under the skin, spreading them evenly.

■ Lay a chicken breast or two thighs on a piece of aluminum foil and wrap loosely. When all the pieces are wrapped, you will have 4 packets. Line a baking tray with 3 layers of aluminum foil. Lay the 4 packets on the tray in pairs, one packet on top of another. Fold the foil lining of the baking tray over the top to make one parcel. Place in the refrigerator overnight so that the chicken marinates thoroughly.

■ Cook in the oven at 325°F for 1 hour, then reduce to 225°F and cook for another 1–2 hours. To serve, unwrap the parcel and packets and put the chicken pieces on dinner plates, or put onto a warm serving dish together with the cooking juices.

■ Serve with rice or noodles or boiled new potatoes and vegetables.

Note: Ayam Betutu can also be eaten cold, sliced thin, with a salad. You can cook duck breasts in the same way, but remember to pour off the surplus oil when you open up the packets.

Padang Fried Chicken

GORENG AYAM BALADO

SERVES 4

Balado is a Minangkabau (West Sumatran) word meaning "with chile." Padang is the port of the Minangkabau country. Nasi Padang nowadays means rice with dishes cooked in the tradition of Padang restaurants. Everything is cooked in advance, and almost everything is chile-hot. In any restaurant that calls itself Rumah Makan Padang you will find 10 or more dishes spread before you, from which you choose and help yourself. You are charged only for what you eat.

Leave out the chiles if you wish, but they will not be excessively hot because the Padang people do not use the strong bird's-eye chiles but the large red chiles, which are really quite mild.

INGREDIENTS

3 tablespoons tamarind water	8–10 large red chiles, seeded and chopped
pinch turmeric	6 shallots or 2 onions, thinly sliced
1 teaspoon salt	2 tablespoons vegetable oil
1/2 teaspoon ground coriander	1/2 teaspoon salt
1/2 teaspoon ground white pepper	vegetable oil for deep-frying
1 2 1/2- to 3-pound chicken, cut into serving pieces	

METHOD

■ To make the marinade, mix together the tamarind water, turmeric, salt, coriander, and pepper in a bowl. Add the chicken pieces, and marinate for 2 hours or overnight in the refrigerator.

■ To make the chile sauce, in a frying pan fry the chiles and shallots or onions in the oil, stirring continuously, for about 5–6 minutes. Add the salt. Set aside.

■ Drain the chicken from the marinade. Discard the marinade. Deep-fry the chicken, a few pieces at a time, until the skin is golden brown and the bones are crisp. Put all the fried chicken in a large bowl and pour the chile sauce over it. Using two large spoons, turn the chicken pieces over and over until they are evenly coated.

■ This dish should be eaten with the fingers, either as a snack or as a main course with fried rice or fried noodles.

METHOD

Chicken in Fragrant Leaves

KAI HO BATEI

SERVES 8 AS
A STARTER, 4
AS A MAIN
COURSE

This is a domestic version of street food that I ate in Bangkok. A cook at my friend's house taught me to make the little envelopes from pandanus leaf, which I found rather tricky at first. She told me the easiest method is simply to put a few strips of pandanus leaf under and on top of the meat, so that you get the flavor, and use aluminum foil for the actual wrapping. Here, I suggest you use paper and serve the parcels still fully wrapped. Your guests can then have the pleasure of undoing them for themselves and being surprised at the delicious fragrance. The pandanus leaves, cooked, are soft and edible—at least, the young ones are.

INGREDIENTS

4 tablespoons chopped cilantro	2 pounds ground chicken meat
2 teaspoons green peppercorns	8 sheets of waxed paper for wrapping, about 12 inches square
4 cloves garlic	
3 teaspoons sugar	4–6 pandanus leaves, cut into 16 strips about 1/2-inch wide
2 tablespoons light soy sauce	
2 tablespoons sesame seeds	vegetable oil for deep-frying
1 teaspoon salt	

METHOD

■ Pound the cilantro, peppercorns, and garlic in a mortar until smooth. Put this paste in a bowl, add the sugar, soy sauce, sesame seeds, and salt. Mix together and add the chicken. Mix well to coat the chicken thoroughly and let marinate for at least 1 hour. (It can be left longer in the refrigerator, if necessary.)

■ Divide the chicken into 8 equal portions. To wrap it, put a square of waxed paper diamond-wise on a flat surface and arrange one portion of chicken, with 2 or 3 strips of pandanus leaf below and on top, not quite in the center of the square—a little closer to you. Fold the corner nearest you to cover the chicken but don't fold the sheet in half—leave a wide margin on the side furthest from you. Fold the left and right corners in across the center. Now fold the section that contains the chicken away from you, so that you make a square packet with a triangular flap sticking out at one corner. Finally fold this flap and tuck it into the pocket made by the previous folds, as if you were closing an envelope.

■ Heat the oil in a wok or deep-frying pan. Fry about 4 packets at a time, for 6 minutes, turning over once. Serve immediately.

Spicy Green Duck

BEBEK HIJAU PANGGANG

SERVES 8 AS
A STARTER OR
4 AS A MAIN
COURSE

This is a variation of a traditional Sumatran duck stew, very hot and green in color because of the number of green chiles used. If you don't like it hot, reduce the chiles or replace them with green bell pepper. I find cooking the duck this way suits Western tastes perfectly, because you get a nice and tender duck and not overcooked, the skin is crispy, and the marinade makes the duck very tasty and juicy. But it is essential to serve this dish straight from the oven. It is suitable for a first course for 8 people, accompanied by watercress with slices of orange or mango, or you can serve it as a main course for 4, with rice and vegetables. For a main course, heat the marinade and use it as a hot sauce.

INGREDIENTS

8 large green chiles, seeded and chopped	4 tablespoons tamarind water or white malt vinegar
12 shallots	
10 candlenuts or raw macadamia nuts	3 kaffir lime leaves or bay leaves
5 cloves garlic	freshly ground black pepper
1/2 stalk lemongrass, outer leaf discarded	1 teaspoon salt
1 2-inch piece ginger	2 tablespoons vegetable oil
1/2 teaspoon turmeric	8 duck breasts
1/2 teaspoon galingal	

METHOD

■ To make the marinade, in a food processor blend the chiles, shallots, candlenuts or macadamia nuts, garlic, lemongrass, and ginger to a smooth paste. Transfer the paste to a bowl, and add the turmeric, galingal, tamarind water or vinegar, kaffir lime leaves or bay leaves, pepper, salt, and oil. Put the pieces of duck in the marinade. Cover the bowl and keep in the refrigerator for at least 2 hours, or preferably overnight.

■ Preheat the oven to 350°F. Drain the duck and place on a rack in a baking tray. (If serving the duck as a main course, transfer the marinade to a saucepan as soon as the duck is in the oven, simmer to reduce until thick, and use as a sauce.) Half fill the tray with hot water and roast in the oven for 35–40 minutes. Serve immediately.

Note: Do not reheat the duck or freeze it cooked. It can, however, be frozen with the marinade before cooking. Thaw it out completely before cooking.

Liver and Tofu in Rich Coconut Cream Sauce

SAMBAL GORENG HATI DAN TAHU

SERVES 4

"Sambal goreng" is a generic name for dishes served all over Indonesia. As with curry, once you have cooked it a few times you can invent endless variations of ingredients. I have always found this combination of liver and tofu very successful. I used to be convinced that the secret of sambal goreng was the candlenuts. But an Indonesian friend, who has given me many recipes, told me she does not use candlenuts, and her sambal goreng is exquisite. So I have marked the candlenuts "optional."

INGREDIENTS

4 shallots	1 pound calf's liver or chicken livers, cut into thin bite-size pieces
1 clove garlic	
3 large red chiles, seeded, or pinch cayenne and 1 teaspoon paprika	1 tablespoon tamarind water or 1 tamarind slice
2 candlenuts or raw macadamia nuts (optional)	1 to 1 1/2 cups thick coconut milk
1 1/2-inch slice shrimp paste	1/2 stalk lemongrass or pinch lemongrass powder
1 1-inch piece ginger	2 kaffir lime leaves or bay leaves
1/2 cup sunflower oil, divided	1/2 pound fried tofu, halved
2 tablespoons water	salt to taste
pinch galingal	1/4 pound sugar snap peas
1 teaspoon ground coriander	1 large tomato, peeled, seeded, and chopped

METHOD

■ To make the paste, put the shallots, garlic, chiles, candlenuts or macadamia nuts, if desired, shrimp paste, and ginger in a blender with 2 tablespoon of the oil and the water, and blend until smooth. Add the coriander and galingal powder to this paste.

■ Heat the remaining oil in a wok or frying pan and fry the liver in 2 or 3 batches for 2 minutes each time. Remove and drain on paper towels.

■ Put 2 tablespoons of the same oil into a saucepan, heat, and fry the paste from the blender, stirring continuously, for 2 minutes. Add the tamarind water or tamarind slice, stir, and add the coconut milk, lemongrass and kaffir lime leaves or bay leaves. Simmer, stirring frequently, for 50 minutes, or until the sauce thickens.

■ Add the liver, tofu, and salt. Continue to simmer for 2 minutes, then add the peas and tomato. Stir for 1–2 minutes, remove the tamarind slice, lemongrass, and kaffir lime leaves or bay leaves. Serve hot with rice.

Liver and Tempeh Croquettes

KROKET HATI DAN TEMPE

MAKES 15–20 CROQUETTES

Tempeh is an Indonesian product, made of fermented soy beans. Although by itself it tastes rather bland, it has a pleasant nutty flavor enhanced by the liver and spices.

INGREDIENTS

1/2 pound tempeh, cubed	2 tablespoons grated palm sugar or brown sugar
4 scallions	2 teaspoons salt
1 onion, chopped	2 cups cold water
2 cloves garlic, chopped	8–12 ounces calf's liver or chicken livers, cubed
1 teaspoon ground coriander	
1/2 teaspoon cayenne	2 eggs, separated
2 tablespoons tamarind water or 2 tamarind slices	vegetable oil for deep-frying

METHOD

■ Put the tempeh in a saucepan with all the other ingredients except the liver, eggs, and oil. Add the cold water, bring to a boil, and simmer for 40–50 minutes, or until most of the water has evaporated.

■ Add the liver, stir, and continue cooking for 2 minutes. Drain off and discard the remaining cooking juices as well as most or all of the solids, leaving just the tempeh and liver. Allow these to cool.

■ When cool, put the tempeh and liver with the egg yolks in a blender and blend to the consistency of a coarse pâté.

■ Form the pâté mixture into 15–20 croquettes. Lightly beat the 2 egg whites in a bowl, and roll each croquette in the egg white before deep-frying. Deep-fry 5 at a time in hot oil for about 3–4 minutes. Serve hot or cold as a snack lunch with salad.

Fried Tripe

GORENG BABAT

SERVES 4–6

Tripe is popular all over Indonesia—and not just because it is cheap. Even if you think you don't like tripe, give this dish a try.

INGREDIENTS

2 tablespoons tamarind water	1/2 cup vegetable oil
1 teaspoon salt	8 shallots, thinly sliced
1/2 teaspoon cayenne	4 green or red chiles, seeded and thinly sliced
2 cloves garlic, crushed	
1 teaspoon ground coriander	2 tablespoons dark soy sauce, preferably Indonesian kecap manis
1 pound cooked and cleaned tripe, cut into 3/4-inch strips	pinches salt

METHOD

■ To make the marinade, mix together the tamarind water, salt, cayenne, garlic, and coriander in a bowl. Add the tripe and marinate it for 2 hours or overnight in the refrigerator. Drain the tripe and discard the marinade.

■ Heat the oil in a wok or frying pan and fry the tripe in batches, for 4–6 minutes each time. Take out with a slotted spoon and drain on paper towels.

■ When all the tripe has been fried, discard all but 1 tablespoon of the oil.

■ To make the sauce, in the same wok or frying pan fry the shallots and chiles, stirring continuously, for 3 minutes. Add the soy sauce. If you are using Indonesian kecap manis, which is rather sweet, add 1–2 large pinches of salt. Stir, and add the fried tripe. Stir, and turn the tripe for 1–2 minutes. Serve at once with boiled rice and cooked vegetables.

RICE AND NOODLE DISHES

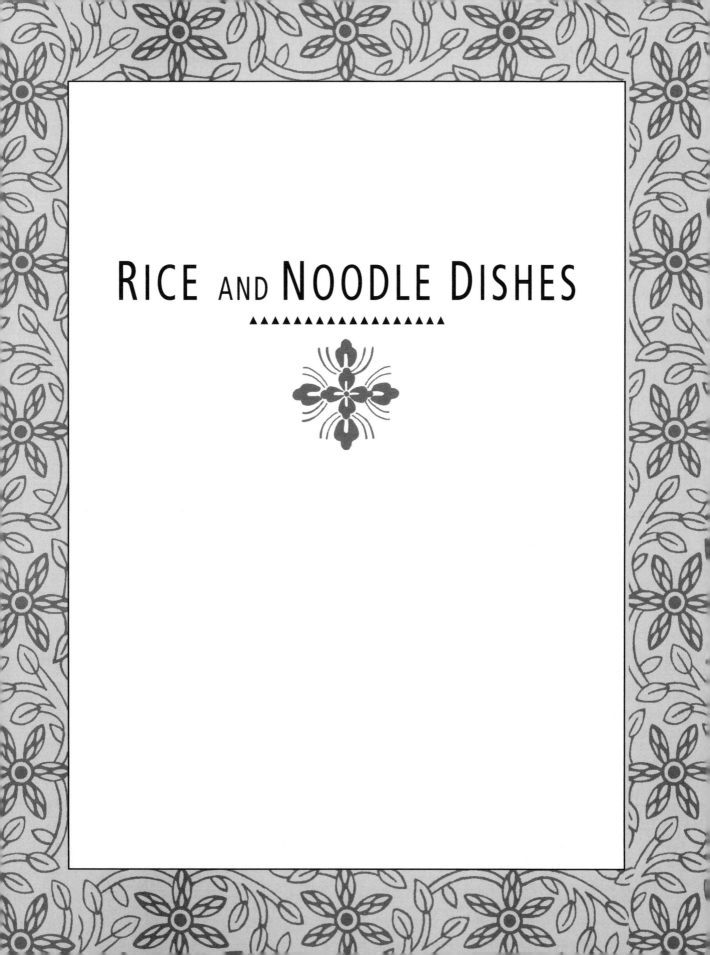

Rice, obviously, is our staple food in Southeast Asia. Noodles, too, play a big part in our diet. The number of different ways of cooking these apparently simple things is enormous. Rice and noodles are found in all sorts of shapes, colors, textures, and flavors and can be cooked in all sorts of ways. A few of the varieties—the ones that will be of immediate use to readers of this book—are listed in the Introduction under "Specialty Ingredients." The recipes that follow will, I hope, help people to realize that cooking this kind of food is not at all difficult, and that it gives scope for improvisation and experimentation.

Much as I like noodles, the story of their manufacture is not very exciting. On the other hand, the cultivation of rice is complex, involving back-breaking work contrasted with the extraordinary beauty of terraced ricefields and the rice itself at every stage of growth.

Terraced ricefields in Bali

Fried Rice

NASI GORENG

SERVES 4–6

Every rice-growing country has its own favorite recipes for savory fried rice. In Indonesia, this is not only deliciously spicy but turns a wonderfully rich red-gold color as well. Here I give you the basic ingredients for Nasi Goreng.

INGREDIENTS

1 1/2 cups long-grain rice	3 medium carrots, diced very small
1 1/2 cups water	1/4 pound button mushrooms, thinly sliced
1 tablespoon vegetable oil	1 teaspoon paprika
1 tablespoon melted butter	1/2 teaspoon cayenne
3 shallots	2 teaspoons tomato purée or tomato ketchup
1 clove garlic (optional)	1 tablespoon light soy sauce
1/4 pound chicken breast, sliced into small pieces	1 teaspoon salt

METHOD

■ Wash the rice once or twice under cold running water and put it in a saucepan, preferably one with a thick bottom and a tight-fitting lid. Add the water, bring to a boil, then simmer, uncovered, until all the water has been absorbed by the rice. Stir the rice once. Cover as tightly as possible so that the steam from the remaining moisture cannot escape. Reduce the heat and continue cooking very slowly for 10 minutes. A little rice will stick to the bottom of the pan; it is easily removed by soaking,

■ Heat the oil and butter in a wok or large frying pan. Fry the shallots and garlic, if desired, for 1–2 minutes, add the chicken, and stir-fry for 2 minutes. Add the carrots and mushrooms and continue stir-frying for 2 more minutes. Add the paprika, cayenne, tomato purée or ketchup, soy sauce, and salt, and stir for 1 minute or more, or until the carrots and mushrooms are cooked. Now add the rice, and mix well by stirring continuously until it is hot. Serve at once.

Note: In Indonesia fried rice is often served with an omelette cut into narrow strips laid on top of it, or with a fried egg for each person and perhaps some watercress and slices of cucumber. It makes an excellent light meal or an accompaniment to the main meal of the day.

Fried Rice with Egg and Scallions

KAO PAHT KHAI

SERVES 4–6

In this version of Thai fried rice, the eggs are scrambled with the rice a few minutes before serving. As with the previous recipe, you can serve this rice as a base for saté or dry-fried meat or vegetable dishes.

INGREDIENTS

2 tablespoons peanut oil

2 large green chiles, seeded and thinly sliced, or 1/2 teaspoon ground white pepper

6 scallions, thinly sliced, white and green parts separated

2 cloves garlic, minced (optional)

6 cups cold boiled rice

1 tablespoon light soy sauce

1 tablespoon fish sauce

pinch salt

2–3 eggs, beaten

2 tablespoons chopped cilantro

METHOD

■ Heat the oil in a wok or saucepan and fry the chiles, the white part of the scallions, and the garlic, if desired, stirring continuously, for 1 minute. Add the rice, stirring continuously again until the rice is hot.

■ Add the soy sauce, fish sauce, and salt, stir, and add the eggs, the green part of the scallions, and the chopped cilantro.

■ Continue stirring vigorously until the eggs are well mixed with the rice and cooked. Serve immediately.

Coconut Rice

NASI LEMAK

SERVES 4–6

Boiling the rice in coconut milk gives it a flavor that everyone seems to like.

INGREDIENTS

1 1/2 cups long-grain rice	1 1/2 cups coconut milk
2 tablespoons vegetable oil or clarified butter	1 teaspoon salt
	1 salam leaf or bay leaf

METHOD

■ Soak the rice in cold water for 1 hour, wash, and drain. Heat the oil or butter in a saucepan and sauté the rice for 3 minutes.

■ Add the coconut milk, salt, and salam leaf or bay leaf, and simmer for about 10 minutes, or until the rice has absorbed all the liquid. Reduce the heat, cover as tightly as possible, and simmer for 10–12 more minutes. Or you can put the half-cooked rice into a rice steamer and steam for 10 minutes. Discard the salam leaf or bay leaf before serving.

Yellow Savory Rice

NASI KUNING

SERVES 4–6

This is a dish for celebrations. Western people often assume that yellow rice must be Indian, but I don't think there is anything exclusively Indian about it.

INGREDIENTS

1 1/2 cups long-grain rice	1 1/2 cups stock or coconut milk
2 tablespoons vegetable oil	1 cinnamon stick
1 teaspoon turmeric	1 clove
1 teaspoon ground coriander	1/2 teaspoon salt
1/2 teaspoon ground cumin	1 salam leaf or bay leaf

METHOD

■ Soak the rice in cold water for 1 hour, wash, and drain. Heat the oil in a saucepan and sauté the rice for 2 minutes.

■ Add the turmeric, coriander, and cumin, and stir-fry for another 2 minutes. Pour in the stock or coconut milk, then add the remaining ingredients. Simmer for about 10 minutes, or until the rice has absorbed all the liquid; then steam for 10 minutes. Or you can cover the saucepan tightly and leave on low heat, undisturbed, for 10 minutes. Discard the salam leaf or bay leaf before serving.

Rice Stuffed with Savory Chicken

AREM-AREM

SERVES 6–8

This dish is lovely for picnics, but equally good served at home as a savory rice cake with saté and vegetables. Wrap the Arem-Arem in banana leaves if you wish.

INGREDIENTS

1 1/2 cups long-grain rice	5 tablespoons very thick coconut milk
pinch salt	1 1/2-inch piece shrimp paste (optional)
5 cups water	2 tablespoons water
2 chicken breasts	4 tablespoons vegetable oil, divided
5 shallots or 1 onion	pinch galingal
3 cloves garlic	1 kaffir lime leaf or bay leaf
3 red chiles, seeded, or 1/2 teaspoon cayenne	1 teaspoon salt
	coconut milk

METHOD

■ Boil the rice in the salted water until the water has been completely absorbed. Stir frequently to keep the rice from sticking to the bottom. Take the pan off the heat and let it cool. The rice will be soft and sticky because it has absorbed so much water.

■ Simmer the chicken breasts for 40 minutes, then shred the meat finely.

■ To make the filling, put the shallots or onion, garlic, chiles, and shrimp paste, if desired, into a blender with the water and half the oil and blend until smooth.

■ In a wok or frying pan, heat the remaining oil and fry this paste, stirring continuously, for 1 minute. Add the galingal, kaffir lime leaf or bay leaf, and salt, stir again, and add the coconut milk. Bring to a boil, and simmer for 30 minutes. Add the shredded chicken, stir for 1–2 minutes, then continue cooking for 5–10 minutes, or until all the coconut milk has been absorbed by the chicken. Taste, add more salt, if necessary, then let cool.

■ When the rice and filling have cooled, put one-third of the rice in a baking dish and flatten it with the back of a spoon. Then put half of the filling on top of the rice and smooth it out in the same way. Repeat with another layer of rice, the rest of the filling, and finally the rest of the rice on top.

■ Cover the dish with aluminum foil if it has no lid, and steam in the oven at 350°F for 40–50 minutes. You can serve this hot or cold.

Mixed Stew with Cellophane Noodles

THOM KHEM

SERVES 6–8

This Thai dish reminds me of our Indonesian *semur*, or *smoor*, as the Dutch used to call it. It is an excellent way of using up leftovers of roast chicken or pork. In Indonesia we would make Egg Semur as a separate dish. Thom Khem has hard-boiled eggs as well as meat. There should be plenty of rich dark brown sauce with this dish.

INGREDIENTS

3 1/2-ounce package cellophane noodles	1/2 pound fresh straw mushrooms, quartered, or 1/2 pound fresh oyster mushrooms, thinly sliced
4 chicken breasts	1/2 teaspoon cayenne or white pepper
4 chicken thighs	3–4 tablespoons dark soy sauce
1/2 pound pork, cubed	1 teaspoon turbinado sugar
3 cups water	1/2 pound mustard greens, roughly chopped
4 shallots, unpeeled	6 oz fried tofu, quartered
4 cloves garlic, unpeeled	4 hard-boiled eggs, halved
2 teaspoons salt	2 tablespoons minced cilantro
2 tablespoons vegetable oil	2 tablespoons minced scallions

METHOD

■ Soak the noodles in hot water for 3 minutes, drain, and chop.

■ Put the chicken and pork in a saucepan. Pour in the water and add the shallots, garlic, and salt. Simmer gently for 40–50 minutes, skimming several times to take the grease off the surface. Take out the meat, shallots, and garlic and allow them to cool. Strain the stock and set aside.

■ When cool, cut the chicken into bite-size pieces, discarding the skin and bones. Do the same for the pork. Peel the shallots and garlic and mash them on a plate with the back of a spoon.

■ In a wok or saucepan, heat the oil and fry the mushrooms, stirring continuously, for 1 minute. Add the mashed shallots and onions, cayenne or pepper, soy sauce, and sugar. Stir and add about 1 cup of the stock. Simmer for 4 minutes, add the mustard greens, then simmer for 2 more minutes.

■ Stir in the chicken, pork, and tofu, adding more stock, if necessary. Simmer for 2 minutes, then add the remaining ingredients. Let this bubble for 1 minute. Serve hot.

Fried Noodles with Seafood

MIE GORENG DENGAN IKAN LAUT

SERVES 4

This is a somewhat elaborate dish. You can just cook the basic fried noodles, without the seafood.

INGREDIENTS

1/2 pound egg noodles	1/2 pound scallops
2 tablespoons vegetable oil	1/2 pound small squid
5 shallots, minced	1/2 pound prawns, peeled
1/2 teaspoon ground ginger	1/2 pound any firm-fleshed fish
1 teaspoon ground coriander	8 tablespoons vegetable oil
2 carrots, sliced	2 shallots, finely sliced
2 cabbage leaves, coarsely shredded	2 cloves garlic, chopped
2 tablespoons light soy sauce	2 tablespoons yellow tauco (yellow bean sauce)
2 tomatoes, peeled, seeded, and chopped	pinch cayenne
4 scallions, minced	
salt and pepper to taste	

METHOD

■ Cook the noodles in boiling salted water for 4–5 minutes, or according to the instructions on the package. Drain and rinse under cold running water for a few seconds. Loosen and shake out the strands a little, then let cool and dry.

■ In a wok or frying pan heat the oil and fry the shallots for 1 minute, then add the ginger and coriander. Stir for a few seconds, add the carrots and cabbage, and continue stirring for about 4 minutes. Add the soy sauce and the noodles, and stir for 3 minutes. Add the tomatoes, scallions, and salt and pepper. Turn and stir for another minute.

■ Clean and prepare the scallops, squid, prawns, and fish. Fry each separately in the oil in a wok or frying pan for 2–3 minutes. Discard all but 2 tablespoons of the oil. Fry the shallots and garlic in it, stirring continuously, for 2 minutes. Stir in the yellow bean sauce and cayenne. Add the seafood, and stir-fry all together for not more than 2 minutes. Arrange on top of the fried noodles. Serve immediately.

Fried Rice Vermicelli

MIEHUN GORENG

SERVES 4

Miehun Goreng is just right for a quick, nourishing lunch, whether you mix it with fish and prawns, with liver and vegetables, or with vegetables alone. Whatever you choose, the method of preparing and stir-frying the noodles and the other ingredients is the same. The recipe that follows is my own particular favorite: liver with leeks.

INGREDIENTS

6-ounce package rice vermicelli	2 tablespoons vegetable oil
1 pound calf's liver or chicken livers	1 1-inch piece ginger, chopped
1/2 pound leeks	pinch cayenne
3 medium carrots	2 tablespoons light soy sauce
1/4 pound mustard greens	salt to taste

METHOD

■ Put the rice vermicelli into a pan of lightly salted boiling water, cover, and let it stand for 2–3 minutes. Drain the vermicelli in a colander and rinse under cold running water for a few seconds. Loosen and shake out the strands of vermicelli a little, then let cool and dry.

■ Slice the liver very thin and cut it into small, bite-size pieces. Cut the leeks down the middle and wash thoroughly. Then slice them diagonally into pieces about 1/2 inch thick. Slice the carrots diagonally as well. Wash the mustard greens and chop them coarsely.

■ Heat the oil in a wok and stir-fry the leeks and carrots for 2 minutes. Add the liver, ginger, and cayenne, and stir-fry for another 3 minutes. Add the soy sauce and greens, and continue stir-frying for 2 more minutes.

■ Add the rice vermicelli, and keep on stirring and turning until all the ingredients are well mixed and the rice vermicelli is hot. Season with salt and serve immediately.

Rice-Stick Noodles with Pork and Bean Sprouts

SEN MEE PUD

SERVES 4

For this recipe, I often use Japanese noodles called *udon*. It's a good dish for finishing off the leftovers of Sunday roast pork, crackling and all.

INGREDIENTS

1/2 pound rice-stick noodles or udon	1 tablespoon fish sauce
2 tablespoons peanut oil	1/2 pound roast pork, thinly sliced
2 shallots, thinly sliced	4 scallions, sliced diagonally
1 1-inch piece ginger, minced	1/4 pound bean sprouts
2 green chiles, seeded and sliced diagonally	2 tablespoons chopped cilantro
2 cloves garlic, crushed	salt and sugar to taste
1 tablespoon light soy sauce	

METHOD

■ Cook the noodles in boiling salted water for 4–5 minutes, or according to the instructions on the package. Drain and rinse under cold running water for a few seconds, then let cool and dry.

■ In a wok or large saucepan, heat the oil. Fry the shallots, ginger, chiles, and garlic for 2 minutes, stirring continuously. Add the soy sauce and fish sauce. Stir-fry for 2 more minutes. Add the pork and scallions, simmer for 2 minutes, then add the bean sprouts and cilantro. Stir-fry for another 2 minutes. Season with salt and sugar.

■ Stir in the noodles and serve immediately. If you have some leftover pork crackling, break it up into small pieces and sprinkle over the noodles.

Crispy Rice Vermicelli

MEE KROB

SERVES 4

This dish must be eaten as soon as it is cooked, and the helpings should be quite small. The meat mixture can be made well in advance, but the egg flakes must be made and mixed at the last moment. The pickled garlic can be bought in small jars or cans, and the grated orange rind is a substitute for *som sa* (page 19).

INGREDIENTS

6-ounce package rice vermicelli	2 tablespoons tamarind water or 1 tablespoon mild vinegar
6 tablespoons vegetable oil, divided	1 tablespoon sugar
2 shallots, sliced	2 teaspoons fish sauce
2 cloves garlic, chopped	2 eggs, lightly beaten
1/4 pound pork, coarsely chopped	4 tablespoons bean sprouts, raw or blanched
2 chicken breasts, coarsely chopped	
1/8 pound shrimp	4 cloves pickled garlic, chopped
1/4 pound fried tofu, quartered (optional)	1 red chile, seeded and thinly sliced
2 tablespoons yellow tauco (yellow bean sauce)	2 tablespoons Goreng Bawang/Fried Shallots (page 141)
	1 tablespoon grated orange rind

METHOD

■ Put the rice vermicelli into a pan of lightly salted boiling water, cover, and let it stand for 2–3 minutes. Drain the vermicelli in a colander and rinse under cold running water for a few seconds. Loosen and shake out the strands of vermicelli a little, then let cool and dry. When dry and cold, fry the vermicelli in several batches in hot oil until crisp.

■ In a wok or frying pan heat 2 tablespoons of the oil and fry the shallots and garlic for 1–2 minutes. Add the pork and chicken and stir-fry for 3 minutes. Then add the shrimp, tofu, if desired, yellow bean sauce, and tamarind water or vinegar. Stir again and simmer for 3 minutes. Add the sugar and fish sauce, and simmer the mixture gently while you fry the egg.

METHOD

■ In a frying pan, heat the remaining oil. With a spoon, dribble the beaten egg continually into the oil; each drop will become a golden flake. Stir and remove with a slotted spoon.

■ Just before serving, mix the crisp vermicelli with the meat mixture and the egg flakes in a large wok over medium heat. Mix and stir for about 2 minutes. This can be done in stages, a portion at a time, if your wok is small.

■ Garnish with the bean sprouts, pickled garlic, chile, Goreng Bawang, and orange rind. Serve immediately.

VEGETABLES, TOFU AND TEMPEH

▲▲▲▲▲▲▲▲▲▲▲▲▲▲▲▲▲▲

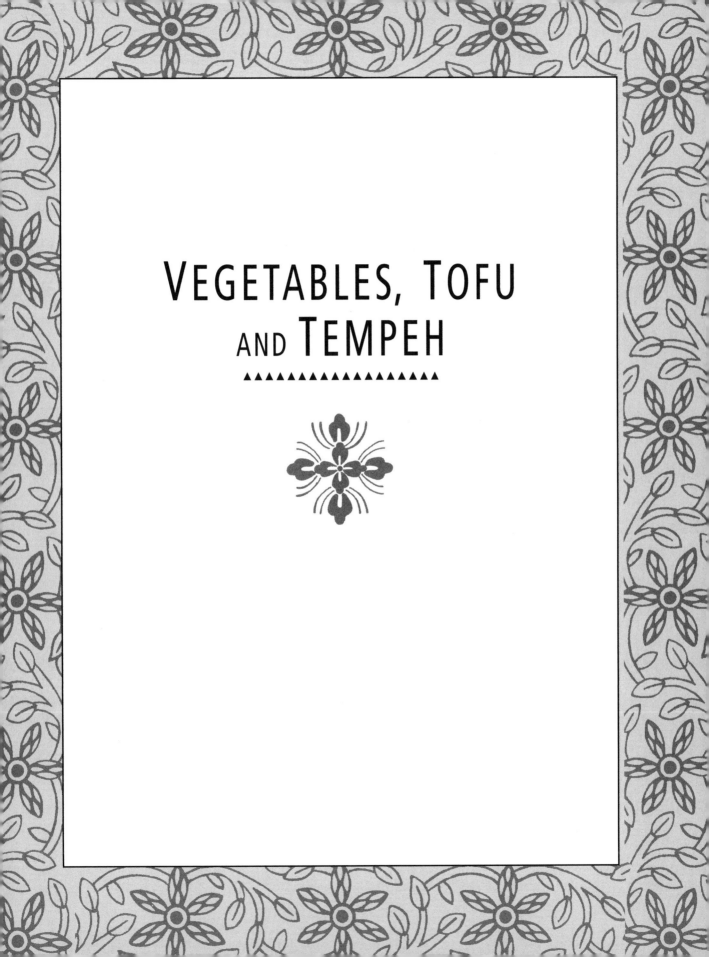

I am sometimes tempted to turn vegetarian when I consider how many good things can be made with vegetables alone. With tofu and tempeh, after all, one need not worry about missing any vital protein or vitamins. I can't quite bring myself yet to abandon meat and fish, but it is certainly no hardship for me to cater for a vegetarian party. Most of the dishes in this section are very lightly cooked, so the ingredients keep their flavor and texture as well as their goodness. Don't assume, however, that this means you needn't start doing anything about the meal until just before you want to eat. Thai and Indonesian food takes, as a rule, much longer to prepare than it does to cook; there is a lot of cleaning and cutting up to be done.

Tofu and tempeh are both made from soy beans. Tofu (tahu in Indonesian) is familiar in Western countries. You can buy it fresh, in which case you submerge it in water and keep it in the refrigerator for, at most, 3 or 4 days; or you can buy packages of "silken" tofu, which is good but a little too soft to be ideal for my purposes. Buying the fresh tofu is really the best.

The Thais don't know anything about tempeh, and many regions of Indonesia itself don't make it and don't like it—my father, who was born and raised in West Sumatra, would never touch it. But the Javanese love it, and as I spent so much of my early life in Java I became fond of it, too.

Bamboo shoot, peppers and chile, diamond-shaped bamboo shoot cuttings

Stir-Fried Bean Sprouts and Sugar Snap Peas

OSENG-OSENG TAUGE DAN ERCIS

SERVES 4

This dish is delicious, attractive and very easy and quick to make. The main ingredients are relatively cheap and available year-round.

INGREDIENTS

1 pound bean sprouts	pinch cayenne or ground white pepper
2 tablespoons sunflower oil	1 tablespoon light soy sauce
2 shallots, thinly sliced	1/2 pound sugar snap peas
1 clove garlic, crushed	1/2 teaspoon salt
1 1-inch piece ginger, minced	large pinch sugar

METHOD

■ Clean the bean sprouts by putting them in a large bowl, filling it with cold water, and then carefully pouring the water out. By doing this several times you will get rid of the green bits of the mung beans that stuck to the sprouts. (I usually pick off and discard the brownish roots of the bean sprouts—a very time-consuming job, but your dish will look much more attractive.)

■ In a wok or large frying pan, heat the oil and fry the shallots, garlic, and ginger for 1 minute, stirring continuously. Add the cayenne or pepper and the soy sauce. Stir, then add the sugar snap peas. Stir for 1 minute and add the bean sprouts. Continue stirring for 2 minutes, then add the salt and sugar and stir again. Serve immediately, or eat cold as a salad.

Black-Eyed Peas in a Coconut Dressing

JUKUT MURAB

SERVES 6–8

This is a Balinese version of a salad, popular all over Java, which makes good use of young, tender coconut for the dressing. Even though the fresh coconuts available in the West are quite old and a bit tough and chewy, you'll be surprised how good this spicy coconut dressing is. If you are a vegetarian this recipe is made just for you.

INGREDIENTS

1 pound black-eyed peas	2 cloves garlic, crushed
2 teaspoons fried shrimp paste (optional)	juice of 1 lime
1 coconut, freshly grated	1 teaspoon brown sugar
4 scallions, thinly sliced	1 teaspoon salt
1 large red chile, seeded	1 cucumber, thinly sliced
1/2 teaspoon cayenne	2 tablespoons chopped mint or basil

METHOD

■ Soak the black-eyed peas in cold water overnight. Wash and drain, then boil them in lightly salted water for 40–50 minutes. Drain again.

■ Put the shrimp paste, if desired, in a bowl, and mash it with the back of a wooden spoon. Add the remaining ingredients except the peas, cucumber, and mint or basil and mix well. Add these final ingredients and mix together thoroughly. Serve cold as a salad.

Steamed Cabbage in a Coconut Dressing

URAP KOL

SERVES 4–6

In Indonesia we consider this an everyday dish for the family. I have served it at dinner parties elsewhere and it is regarded as rather exotic. No doubt it was the freshly grated coconut that did it.

INGREDIENTS

1 pound cabbage, shredded	1/2 teaspoon cayenne
2 teaspoons fried shrimp paste	1 teaspoon brown sugar (optional)
2 cloves garlic, crushed	1 teaspoon salt
juice of 1 lime	1 coconut, freshly grated

METHOD

■ Steam the shredded cabbage for 3 minutes. Keep it warm.

■ Put the fried shrimp paste on a plate, and mash it with the back of a wooden spoon. Add the garlic, lime juice, cayenne, sugar, if desired, and salt. Mix well. Then add this paste mixture to the grated coconut. Mix well again, adding more salt, if necessary.

■ Dress the steamed cabbage with the coconut dressing. Serve warm or cold.

Sweet Salad of Carrots and Daikon

ASINAN WORTEL DENGAN LOBAK

SERVES 4–6

This is a simple but very refreshing salad.

INGREDIENTS

1/2 pound carrots	1 teaspoon salt
1/2 pound daikon	1 red chile, seeded and thinly sliced, or pinch cayenne
3 tablespoons white distilled vinegar	
5 tablespoons warm water	1 green chile, seeded and thinly sliced
1 tablespoon sugar	2 shallots, thinly sliced

METHOD

■ Cut the carrots and daikon into very fine matchsticks.

■ Mix the vinegar, water, sugar, and salt in a bowl. Beat with a fork until the sugar and salt dissolve. Add the remaining ingredients and mix well. Serve cold.

Note: This salad will keep in the refrigerator for 2–3 days. It is equally good if you substitute bean sprouts for the daikon; you then have Asinan Wortel Dengan Taugé.

Mixed Cooked Vegetable Salad with Peanut Sauce

PECEL

SERVES 4–6

Pecel is pronounced *p'tsh'l*—an Indonesian c is like ch in "church." As a dish, this is similar to the better-known Gado-Gado, but simpler.

INGREDIENTS

1/2 cup vegetable oil	1 1/2 cups water
1/4 pound raw peanuts	juice of 1/2 a lemon
1 clove garlic, minced	1/4 pound cabbage, shredded
2 shallots, thinly sliced	1/4 pound string beans, cut into thirds
1 1/2-inch piece shrimp paste	1/4 pound carrots, thinly sliced into rounds
salt to taste	
1/2 teaspoon cayenne	1/4 pound cauliflower, cut into florets
1/2 teaspoon brown sugar	1/4 pound bean sprouts (optional)

METHOD

■ To make the sauce, heat the oil in a frying pan and fry the peanuts for 4 minutes. Remove with a slotted spoon and drain in a colander. Let them cool. Grind the peanuts into a fine powder, using a blender or pestle and mortar. Discard the oil except for 1 tablespoon.

■ Crush the garlic, shallots, and shrimp paste in a pestle and mortar, with a little salt. Fry in the remaining oil for 1 minute. Add the cayenne, sugar, more salt, if desired, and the water. Bring to a boil and stir in the ground peanuts. Simmer for 4–6 minutes, stirring occasionally, until the sauce becomes thick. Add the lemon juice and set aside.

■ Boil each vegetable separately for 3–4 minutes. Drain and arrange on a serving plate. Heat the sauce and pour it over the vegetables. Serve hot or warm.

■ If necessary, this can be prepared and mixed together in advance, then heated in a microwave for 1–2 minutes on full power.

Stuffed Eggplants

TERUNG ISI

SERVES 4 AS A STARTER

Several different kinds of eggplant grow in Indonesia and Thailand, and each country has its own ways of cooking them. In Indonesia we often stuff them with minced lamb.

INGREDIENTS

2 large or 4 medium eggplants	1 teaspoon black peppercorns
2 tablespoons salt	2 fresh kaffir lime leaves, shredded, or dried kaffir lime leaves, crushed
1/2 pound okra, or 1 medium eggplant	
vegetable oil for deep frying	pinch galingal
2 tablespoons olive oil	salt to taste
2 medium onions, sliced	1 tablespoon tamarind water or lemon juice
4 cloves garlic, minced	
2 red or green chiles, seeded and cut diagonally	2 teaspoons brown sugar (optional)
	4 tablespoons chopped Italian parsley
2 teaspoons roasted coriander	

METHOD

■ Halve the eggplants lengthwise. Make 2 deep slashes, lengthwise then crosswise, on the exposed surface of each half. Sprinkle these liberally with the salt. Put them in a colander upside down; leave them for 30–50 minutes, then wash the salt off under cold water. Pat the eggplants dry with paper towels. If you are planning to stuff the large eggplants with a medium eggplant (instead of the okra), cut it into julienne strips, sprinkle it with salt, and let it stand for 30–50 minutes. Wash and drain. If you use okra, cut each pod into 3–4 pieces.

■ In a wok or large frying pan heat the oil. When smoke rises, fry the half-eggplants 2 at a time, for 3 minutes each time, turning them once. Put on paper towels to drain off as much oil as possible. When all the eggplant halves are fried, fry the julienne strips of eggplant in the same oil for 2 minutes, stirring continuously. Remove with a slotted spoon to drain. Now, with a spoon, carefully so as not to damage the skin, scoop out the flesh from the eggplant halves, chop roughly, and set aside.

■ Discard the oil and wipe the wok or frying pan to remove the bits of eggplant. Add the 2 tablespoons oil, heat, and fry the onions, stirring continuously, for 3 minutes. Add the garlic, chiles, coriander, peppercorns, kaffir lime leaves, and galingal. Stir, and add the chopped eggplant flesh and strips, or the okra. Continue cooking, stirring continuously. Add the salt, tamarind water or lemon juice, and sugar, if desired. Keep stirring and turning for about 2 minutes, then add the parsley, mixing it well into the eggplants. Remove from the stove.

■ Divide the filling into 4 or 8, and fill the eggplant halves. Arrange in a baking dish and cook in the oven at 350°F for 30–40 minutes. Serve hot or cold.

Stuffed Bitter Melon

KEMBU PARIA

SERVES 4-8

If you like cooking exotic foreign vegetables, try this one. Despite the name, bitter melons taste very good, particularly with this coconut stuffing. If you want a vegetarian dish, leave out the ground meat.

INGREDIENTS

4 medium bitter melons

2 tablespoons salt

8 tablespoons freshly grated coconut

2 tablespoons vegetable oil

4 shallots, thinly sliced

1 clove garlic, thinly sliced

5 tablespoons ground beef, chicken, or pork (optional)

1/2 teaspoon cayenne or ground white pepper

pinch ground nutmeg

pinch turmeric

1 egg, beaten

2 medium potatoes, boiled, peeled, and mashed

salt to taste

2 cups thick coconut milk

METHOD

■ Cut the bitter melons in half lengthwise, then scoop out and discard the seeds. Sprinkle them with salt and set them upside down in a colander for at least 1 hour. Rinse off the salt under cold water, then boil the melon for 4 minutes. Drain.

■ In a dry wok or frying pan, stir-fry the grated coconut until golden brown. Then grind it finely with a pestle and mortar. Set aside.

METHOD

■ To make the stuffing, heat the oil in a wok or frying pan and fry the shallots and garlic for 1 minute, stirring continuously. Add the ground meat, if desired, stir, then add the cayenne or pepper, nutmeg, and turmeric. Stir again, then add the egg and potatoes. Mix everything well and season with salt. Allow to cool, divide into 8 portions, and use these to fill the bitter melons.

■ Now arrange the stuffed melons in a large saucepan. Pour the coconut milk on top of the melons, sprinkle the ground roasted coconut over the top, and simmer for 10–15 minutes until the sauce is thick. Serve hot.

String Beans in Thick Candlenut Sauce

TERIK BUNCIS

SERVES 4

This is an Indonesian sauce.

INGREDIENTS

1 1/2-inch slice shrimp paste (optional)	2 tablespoons water
4 shallots	1 teaspoon ground coriander
4 candlenuts or raw macadamia nuts	1/2 teaspoon ground cumin
1 large red chile, seeded, or 1/2 teaspoon cayenne	1 cup coconut milk
2 cloves garlic	1 kaffir lime leaf or bay leaf
2 tablespoons vegetable oil	1 pound string beans, cut into 1/2-inch pieces
	1 teaspoon salt

METHOD

■ Put the shrimp paste, if desired, shallots, candlenuts or macadamia nuts, chile, and garlic into a blender. Add the oil and water. Blend until smooth. Remove the paste to a small bowl and add the coriander and cumin.

■ Heat the coconut milk in a saucepan with the paste and the kaffir lime or bay leaf. When it starts to boil, stir and let it simmer until the liquid is reduced by half. Add the beans and salt and let this bubble gently, stirring occasionally, for 10 minutes.

■ Taste, and add salt, if necessary, and continue cooking until the beans are well cooked. Transfer to a serving dish and serve hot.

Tempeh Fritters

PERGEDEL TEMPE

**MAKES ABOUT
20 FRITTERS**

Tempeh has no obvious taste of its own, although the rhizopus spores that bind it together do give it a pleasant, very mild, nutty flavor. But it is an excellent base for absorbing and blending strong and subtle flavors, as here.

INGREDIENTS

5 shallots, sliced	1 teaspoon ground coriander
2 cloves garlic, sliced	1/2 teaspoon cayenne
1 tablespoon vegetable oil	3 tablespoons thick coconut milk
14 oz tempeh, minced	2 eggs, divided
6 scallions, thinly sliced	salt to taste
2 tablespoons chopped Italian parsley	vegetable oil for deep-frying

METHOD

■ In a frying pan, fry the shallots and garlic in the oil until soft and lightly browned. In a bowl, mix the tempeh with the fried shallots and garlic, scallions, parsley, coriander, cayenne, coconut milk, and 1 egg. Season with salt.

■ Form this mixture into small balls about the size of a ping-pong ball. Beat the remaining egg in a bowl. Flatten the tempeh balls slightly between the palms of your hands, then dip quickly in the beaten egg. In a wok or deep-fryer, fry the fritters for 3-5 minutes, a few at a time.

■ Serve hot with boiled rice.

Spicy Fried Tofu

GORENG TAHU BERBUMBU

MAKES ABOUT 20 SLICES

A vegetarian friend of mine in Bandung served me this dish as part of our lunch. I then served it as a starter to a fish dinner, and have found it very popular with non-vegetarians as well. Tofu is rather bland; the spices give it some flavor.

INGREDIENTS

4 shallots, finely sliced	1 teaspoon ground coriander
3 tablespoons peanut oil	4 tablespoons rice flour or all-purpose flour
1 pound tofu	1 1/2 teaspoons salt
4 scallions, thinly sliced	4 eggs, beaten, divided
2 red chiles, seeded and chopped	vegetable oil for deep-frying
2 tablespoons minced Italian parsley	

METHOD

■ In a frying pan, fry the shallots in the oil until soft and lightly browned. Drain and let cool.

■ In a bowl, mash the tofu with a fork or potato masher. Add the shallots and the remaining ingredients except 2 of the eggs. Mix well, then pack the mixture into an oblong glass dish. Steam for 15 minutes. Allow to cool a little, and turn out onto a plate.

■ When completely cold, cut into slices about 1 inch thick. Dip each slice into the remaining eggs, and deep-fry for about 3 minutes. Serve hot or cold on crispy lettuce leaves, with Sambal Kacang/Peanut Sauce (page 143) or Nam Chim/Sweet and Sour Chile Sauce (page 145).

Stuffed Tofu

TAHU ISI SAYURAN

SERVES 4

Indonesian tofu is usually stuffed with minced chicken and prawns, but here I used a mixed vegetables stuffing.

Fried tofu becomes moist and soft in a sauce and absorbs flavors most deliciously. This dish is particularly good if you steam the tofu in the sauce, or simmer it with the sauce in a saucepan. I have chosen a simple tomato sauce, garnished with yellow bell peppers and sugar snap peas.

INGREDIENTS

3 medium carrots	water
handful sugar snap peas	4 tomatoes
1/4 pound oyster mushrooms or other mushrooms	1 tablespoon vegetable oil
1 tablespoon vegetable oil	3 shallots, thinly sliced
2 scallions, thinly sliced	1 1-inch piece ginger, minced
2 cloves garlic, thinly sliced	pinch cayenne
1/4 pound bean sprouts	1/2 teaspoon ground coriander
salt and pepper to taste	1 tablespoon light soy sauce
1 1/2-pound package fried tofu, cut into 16–18 pieces	salt and sugar to taste
3 cloves garlic	1 yellow bell pepper, seeded and cut into diamond shapes, blanched
	handful sugar snap peas, blanched

METHOD

■ To make the filling, cut the carrots, sugar snap peas, and mushrooms into short, thin matchsticks. Heat the oil in a wok or saucepan, add the scallions and garlic, stir-fry for 2 minutes, add the bean sprouts and vegetables, and continue stir-frying for about 2 more minutes. Season with salt and pepper. Let cool.

■ With a pair of scissors, cut one side off each tofu cake but do not remove it completely. Scoop out the white tofu from inside with a spoon, chop, and mix with the vegetables.

■ Divide the filling among the tofu cubes. Close them, and arrange in a large saucepan or on a dish that will fit inside your steamer.

METHOD

■ To make the sauce, put the garlic in a saucepan of water that is just boiling; simmer for 5 minutes, add the tomatoes, and simmer for another 5 minutes. Meanwhile, in a small saucepan, heat the oil and fry the shallots for a few minutes. Add the ginger, stir for a minute, then add the cayenne and coriander. Sieve the tomatoes and garlic into the pan. Stir, add the soy sauce, and season with salt and sugar.

■ Pour the sauce over the stuffed tofu, and finally simmer for 5–6 minutes. Garnish with yellow bell peppers and sugar snap peas. Serve hot.

Thai Mango Salad with Pork

YAM MAMUANG

SERVES 4–6

In Indonesia a fruit salad like this would not be mixed with meat. I tasted a mango salad with meat in Bangkok and liked it very much. If you are a vegetarian you can of course leave out the meat. The best mangoes for this dish are half-ripe ones, still hard but already turning yellow.

INGREDIENTS

2 large half-ripe mangoes, cut into julienne strips

1/2 teaspoon salt

1 tablespoon sugar

juice of 1 lime or lemon

2 tablespoons peanut oil

1/2 pound pork tenderloin, cut into strips

2 shallots, thinly sliced

2 cloves garlic, chopped

3 tablespoons fish sauce

1 tablespoon mild vinegar

4 scallions, thinly sliced

2 dried red chiles, seeded and coarsely chopped, or 1/2 teaspoon cayenne

3 tablespoons roasted peanuts, coarsely crushed

salt to taste

METHOD

■ Put the mango into a bowl with the salt, sugar, and lime or lemon juice. Mix well.

■ In a wok or frying pan, heat the oil and fry the pork, stirring continuously, for 3 minutes. Remove with a slotted spoon and drain on paper towels.

■ In the same oil, fry the shallots and garlic for 1 minute, and add the fish sauce, vinegar, scallions, and chiles or cayenne. Stir and add the mango and pork; stir again and remove from the heat. Put everything into a bowl, add the peanuts and salt, and mix well. Allow to cool, then chill in the refrigerator. Serve cold.

Tofu Salad

KETOPRAK

SERVES 2

This is a favorite lunch in Central Java. You can find it in many open-sided cafés where young students gather because the food is good and cheap.

INGREDIENTS

1/2 cup peanut oil	2 tablespoons chopped Italian parsley
2 cakes tofu, each cut into 6 pieces	8 or more tablespoons Sambal Kacang/Peanut Sauce (page 143)
1/4 pound bean sprouts	
salt to taste	8–10 emping crackers (page 147)
2 medium potatoes, peeled and thinly sliced	1 tablespoon Goreng Bawang/Fried Shallots (page 141)
1/4 cucumber, peeled and sliced	

METHOD

■ In a nonstick frying pan, heat the oil and fry the tofu for about 5 minutes, turning them over once. Remove with a slotted spoon and drain in a colander.

■ Clean the bean sprouts and put them in a bowl. Pour boiling water over them with a little salt. Cover and leave for 3 minutes, then drain and keep them warm. In the same oil, fry the potatoes until crisp.

■ To serve, arrange the fried tofu on serving plates with the potatoes, slices of cucumber, and bean sprouts. Top with the parsley. Pour as much sauce as you like on top, crush or break the emping over it, and sprinkle on some fried shallots or onions as well.

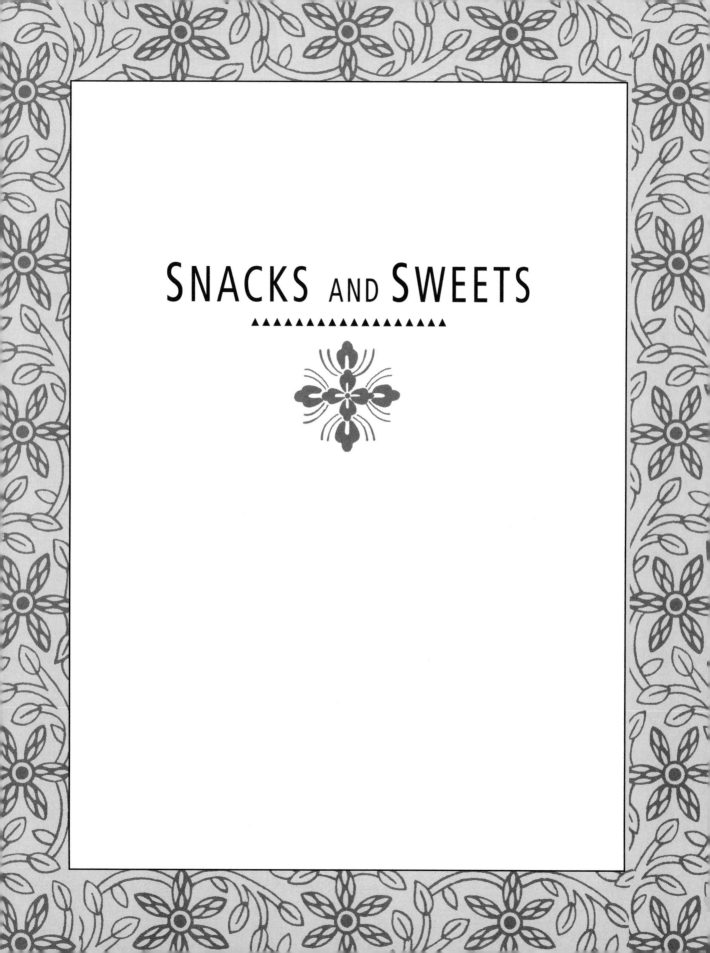

SNACKS AND SWEETS

▲▲▲▲▲▲▲▲▲▲▲▲▲▲▲▲▲

This section covers food for picnics as well as snacks and some sweet things that round off a meal. Southeast Asian cuisines are not as distinguished for sweets as they are for savory dishes. For example, the Javanese have a sweet tooth and consume huge amounts of sugar, probably far more than is good for them, but they have never evolved a large repertoire of sweets or puddings, and their confectioners' shops and pâtisseries rely heavily on Dutch recipes. Nevertheless, there are some good things that deserve to be included here.

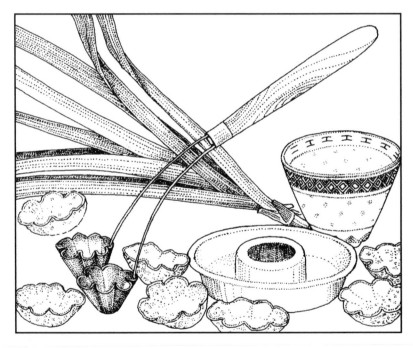

Kratong thong scoop, ready-made kratong thong, pandanus leaf, putu manis cups

Quail Egg "Flowers"

DOK MAI KHAI NOK KRA TA

MAKES 12 "FLOWERS"

The Thais usually make these with miniature or pickling cucumbers, about as big as large gherkins. I sometimes use red radishes, which are easy to cut into "flowers." With a little practice, you can cut flowers out of carrots, chiles, and many other vegetables. Quail egg flowers do take a little time to prepare, but if you are as fond of quail eggs as I am, then the time is well spent.

INGREDIENTS

6 small cucumbers or 12 radishes	2 cloves garlic, chopped
1 cup water	1 tablespoon vegetable oil
2 tablespoons vinegar	pinch ground white pepper
1/2 teaspoon salt	pinch salt
2 tablespoons sugar	1 tablespoon sugar
12 quail eggs	4 tablespoons dark soy sauce
1 tablespoon chopped cilantro	12 cocktail sticks

METHOD

■ Cut the radishes, or whatever vegetables you use to make the "flowers." (Putting the cut shapes into ice water often makes them open further.) If you use small cucumbers, cut them in half, hollow them out to a depth of about 1 inch, and cut the thin sides into petal shapes.

■ To make the marinade, mix together the water, vinegar, salt, and sugar in a bowl. Add the cucumbers or radishes and marinate for 30 minutes.

■ Meanwhile, boil the eggs in salted water for 4 minutes. Drain and peel.

■ In a frying pan, fry the cilantro and garlic in the oil for 1 minute. Add the pepper, salt, sugar, and soy sauce. Stir for another minute. Strain through a sieve into a small bowl. Put the eggs in and marinate for about 2 minutes, turning them several times until they are all evenly brown.

■ Put each egg into the petals of a cucumber flower, and pierce with a cocktail stick "stem" to hold them together. Serve immediately.

Golden Cups

KRATONG THONG

MAKES 50–60 "CUPS"

Puff pastry cups will do very well in this recipe. I recently tasted the most delicious kratong thong fillings served on crispy lettuce leaves at a restaurant. Everything was just right: the minced pork, the peanuts, cilantro, and chile. On the menu they were described as a "Thai pork appetizer." Served as a first course, the lettuce leaves are ideal, but as party snacks the puff pastry cups are more practical. My recipe was given to me by a good friend in Bangkok; it uses chicken instead of pork.

INGREDIENTS

1/2 cup rice flour or all-purpose flour	1 pound boneless chicken breast, minced
2 teaspoons olive oil	pinch cayenne or ground white pepper
3/4 cup cold water	4 tablespoons minced cilantro
1/2 teaspoon salt	1 teaspoon salt
1/2 teaspoon sugar	1/2 teaspoon sugar
vegetable oil for deep-frying	2 teaspoons light soy sauce
1/4 pound roasted unsalted peanuts	2 teaspoons fish sauce (optional)
2 tablespoons vegetable oil	1 tablespoon chopped cilantro
1 large onion, minced	4–6 small red chiles, seeded and minced
3 cloves garlic, minced	

METHOD

■ To make the batter, put the flour in a bowl. Make a well in the middle, pour in the oil. and start mixing the oil and flour with a wooden spoon while gradually adding the water. Mix vigorously until all the water is used. Add the salt and sugar and mix again.

■ The best way to make the golden cups is to use a deep-fryer with a thermostat because you need to keep the oil temperature between 350°–400°F. Heat the oil to this temperature and put the mold for the cups in the oil for about 4 minutes. Dip the outside of the hot scoop up to the brim in the batter and leave it there for 10 seconds. Don't let any batter overflow into the scoop. A layer of batter will start to cook and will adhere to the bottom of the scoop. Now plunge the scoop into the hot oil. Hold it there for 10 seconds before shaking the batter "cups" off the scoop. (You may need to give them a push with a spoon to free them.) Now you have 2 nice golden cups. Remove with a slotted spoon to drain on a plate lined with paper towels.

METHOD

■ Continue as before until all the batter is used up. This batter will make about 50–60 golden cups. When cool, store in an airtight container for later use. They will keep crisp for about 1 week provided the container is really airtight.

■ To make the filling, chop the peanuts the same size as the chicken. Heat the oil in a wok or large frying pan and fry the onion and garlic, stirring continuously, until they are soft. Add the chicken, cayenne or white pepper, and cilantro, stir-fry for about 3 minutes, then add the salt, sugar, soy sauce, and fish sauce.

■ Continue cooking, stirring occasionally, for 4 minutes. Add the peanuts and stir continuously for 1 minute. Adjust the seasoning and let cool. Just before serving, fill the cups and garnish with the cilantro and chiles.

■ To serve as a starter, pile about 2 tablespoons of this filling on top of a crispy lettuce leaf. Serve 3 of these per person. Leave out the chopped chiles in the garnish if you don't like it hot.

Sweet Corn Fritters with Eggplant

PERGEDEL JAGUNG DENGAN TERUNG

MAKES 15–18 FRITTERS

This is a delicious snack, very easy to make, and as good for picnics as it is for parties. Some people prefer them hot, others cold, but I have never met anyone who doesn't want more.

INGREDIENTS

6 fresh ears of corn or 3/4 cup canned corn kernels	2 cloves garlic, chopped
1 medium eggplant	1 teaspoon ground coriander
salt	3 tablespoons rice flour or all-purpose flour
7 tablespoons vegetable oil, divided	1 teaspoon baking powder
4 shallots, chopped	2 tablespoons chopped scallions
1 red chile, seeded and chopped, or 1/2 teaspoon cayenn	1 large egg

METHOD

■ If you are using fresh corn, grate the corn off the cobs. If canned corn is used, drain and put into a bowl, then mash it a little with a wooden spoon to break the kernels so they won't pop when fried. Or you can put them in a blender and blend for a few seconds.

■ Cut the eggplant into very small cubes, put them in a colander, and sprinkle generously with salt. Leave for 30 minutes to 1 hour, rinse off the salt, and squeeze out the excess water. Heat 2 tablespoons of the oil in a wok or frying pan, and fry the shallots, chile, and garlic, stirring them for 1–2 minutes. Add the eggplant, stir, and season with coriander and salt. Simmer, stirring often, for 4 minutes. Remove from the heat and let cool.

■ When cool, put the eggplant mixture, corn, flour, baking powder, and scallions in a bowl. Mix thoroughly and add the egg. Mix well again, taste, and add more salt, if necessary.

■ In a frying pan, heat the remaining oil. Drop a heaped tablespoon of the mixture into the pan. Flatten it with a fork, and repeat this process until you have 5 or 6 pergedel in the pan. Fry them for about 3 minutes on each side, turning once. Serve hot or cold as a snack or as finger food at a party.

Savory Fish Cakes

TOD MAN (PLA KRAI)

MAKES 15-20 FISH CAKES

This is sometimes spelled Tod Mun. Some add the name of the fish it is most often made with in Thailand and call it Tod Man Pla Krai. My recipe was given to me by Thai Chef Mongkol Puntar. I use less cilantro than he does.

INGREDIENTS

5 shallots, chopped	2 teaspoons light soy sauce
4 cloves garlic, chopped	1/2 teaspoon salt
3 red chiles, seeded and chopped	1/4 teaspoon pepper
3 tablespoons chopped cilantro	2 tablespoons olive oil
4 fresh kaffir lime leaves, shredded, or dried kaffir lime leaves, crushed	2 pounds white fish (snapper or cod), diced
handful string beans, sliced into thin rounds	vegetable oil for deep-frying
2 teaspoons sugar	

METHOD

▪ Mix the ingredients in a bowl. Let marinate for 30–40 minutes, or overnight in the refrigerator.

▪ Mince the marinated fish in a food processor.

▪ Take about 1 tablespoon of the fish, put it on the palm of your hand, and form it into a ball. Make all the fish into balls in the same way. The fish balls can be stored in the refrigerator for 1–2 days.

▪ To cook, flatten the fish balls by pressing them gently on a flat surface. Then deep-fry 5 or 6 at a time for 2–3 minutes in a wok or deep-fryer. Take them out with a slotted spoon and drain on paper towels. Serve hot or warm as a snack.

125

Bean Sprout and Fish Fritters

BAKWAN IKAN

**MAKES ABOUT
20 FRITTERS**

Bakwan is one of the many snacks that hawkers sell from house to house in towns in Java. They pass your house several times during the day, each with his characteristic cry.

This is my version of Bakwan, somewhat lighter than the fritters the hawkers sell. I love making these for cocktail parties. Any boned fish can be used, but my favorite is salmon. Leftover cuts or trimmings from salmon fillets are perfect for this recipe.

INGREDIENTS

1/2 pound fish, chopped	4 scallions, thinly sliced
1/2 pound bean sprouts	3 cloves garlic, minced
1/2 cup rice flour or all-purpose flour	1 1-inch piece ginger, chopped
2 teaspoons baking powder	1 teaspoon light soy sauce
1 teaspoon ground coriander	1 teaspoon salt
pinch turmeric	2 small eggs, beaten
2 red or green chiles, seeded and minced	vegetable oil for deep-frying

METHOD

■ In a bowl, mix together all the ingredients except the oil. Heat the oil in a deep skillet or wok to 350°F. With a fork, pick up a little of the batter and drop it into the hot oil. Do this 6 or 8 times, frying each for about 3 minutes.

■ Remove the fritters with a slotted spoon and drain on paper towels. Repeat this process until all the batter has been used up. Serve hot or cold. These can also be served with Nam Chim/Sweet and Sour Chile Sauce (page 145) as a dip.

Savory Pancakes with Chicken and Bamboo Shoot Filling

MARTABAK ISI AYAM DAN REBUNG

MAKES ABOUT 20 PANCAKES

These are not strictly pancakes; they are envelopes of very thin dough, stuffed with ground meat and spices and then quickly fried. The original Martabak from India uses ground beef or lamb for the filling. My version here is filled with chicken and bamboo shoots. They are versatile, good as a snack or as part of a meal.

INGREDIENTS

1 tablespoon olive oil or corn oil

2 large onions, thinly sliced

2 cloves garlic, crushed

1 teaspoon ground coriander

1/2 teaspoon ground cumin

1 teaspoon ground ginger or chopped fresh ginger

1 teaspoon cayenne or freshly ground black pepper

1/2 teaspoon turmeric

1 teaspoon lemongrass powder or 2-inch piece fresh lemongrass, minced

1 pound ground chicken

1/2 cup canned bamboo shoots, diced very small

salt to taste

3 eggs, beaten

4 scallions, thinly sliced

1 4-ounce package wonton wrappers

5 tablespoons vegetable oil for frying

METHOD

■ To make the filling, heat the oil in a wok or frying pan and fry the onions and garlic until soft. Add the spices, fry for another half-minute, stirring continuously, then stir in the ground chicken and bamboo shoots. Fry, stirring occasionally, for about 15 minutes. Season with salt. Let the mixture cool for 30 minutes to an hour. Put the mixture in a bowl, and add the eggs and scallions. Mix well. Put aside the empty wok.

■ To fill the martabak, lay out a few wonton wrappers on a pastry board. Put a tablespoon of filling into half of each wonton square. Then fold the other half over the filling and press the edges down so that they are more or less sealed.

■ Wipe out the same wok and heat the oil to a high temperature. Fry the filled martabak, 5–6 at a time, for about 2 minutes each side; turn once only. The casing should be quite crisp around the edges, but not in the middle, and the finished martabak should be flat and evenly filled with meat almost to the edge. Serve hot or cold.

Mung Bean Savory Chips

REMPEYEK KACANG HIJAU

MAKES 50–60 SAVORY CHIPS

I don't think you can find a more delicious chip than this Indonesian rempeyek. At first glance you might think the recipe is difficult to make, but I assure you it is not at all tricky. You need the Oriental rice powder for this, as the rice flour you get at the supermarket is not fine enough.

INGREDIENTS

1/4 pound mung beans, soaked overnight	1 teaspoon salt
2 candlenuts or raw macadamia nuts	1/4 pound rice powder
1 clove garlic	1 cup cold water
2 teaspoons ground coriander	vegetable oil for frying

METHOD

■ Drain the mung beans.

■ Pound the candlenuts or macadamia nuts and garlic together and place in a bowl. Mix in the coriander, salt, and rice powder, then add the water, a little at a time, stirring and mixing thoroughly. Add the mung beans to the batter.

■ To fry rempeyek, you need a nonstick frying pan and a wok. Heat oil in the frying pan, and also in the wok, sufficient to deep-fry the rempeyek. Take 1 tablespoon of the batter with some beans in it, and pour it quickly into the frying pan. Fry it there for 1–2 minutes—you will probably be able to do 6–7 rempeyek at a time—and then drop the half-cooked rempeyek into the hot oil in the wok. Deep-fry them a few minutes until they are crisp and golden. Continue until all the batter and the beans are used up. Drain and let cool. Store in an airtight container for up to 2 weeks.

Layered Steamed Rice-Flour Cake

KUE LAPIS

MAKES ONE 8-INCH CAKE

Like Lapis Legit/Indonesian Cinnamon Layer Cake (page 133), this steamed cake is time-consuming to make. However, it looks exotic, is very inexpensive, and tastes delicious. I recommend it especially for a large buffet, although you can make a small Kue Lapis as well. In Indonesia you can buy Kue Lapis from street vendors who specialize in them, and we eat slices as a snack at any time. The usual colors are green and white, often with layers of red as well.

INGREDIENTS

2 pandanus leaves, fresh or frozen	1/2 cup sugar
4 tablespoons cold water	1 cup rice flour
3 cups very thick coconut milk	1/3 cup corn flour
pinch salt	

METHOD

■ To make the pandanus juice, put the leaves and water in a blender. Blend for a few seconds, then pass through a fine sieve into a bowl. You will now have about 3 tablespoons of green, fragrant liquid.

■ In a saucepan heat the coconut milk, salt, and sugar, almost to the boiling point, stirring to dissolve the sugar. Remove from the heat and allow to cool a little. Sift the rice flour and corn flour into a bowl. Gradually pour in the lukewarm coconut milk, stirring until you get a smooth, thick batter. Divide this batter between 2 bowls, and put the pandanus juice into one of them. Stir until you get an even green color.

■ Heat a steamer or a double boiler. When the water in the bottom pan is boiling, heat an 8-inch round pan for 2 minutes. Pour in the white batter to make a layer about 1/4-inch thick or less. Steam for 2 minutes, then add the same thickness of green batter and steam for 2 minutes, then add more layers alternately.

■ When all the batter is used up, cover and continue cooking for 3–4 minutes. Cool the cake slightly before turning out onto a plate. When cold cut into about 20 small, thin slices. Serve with tea or coffee after dinner.

Pomegranate and Coconut Cream Agar-Agar

AGAR DELIMA SERIKAYA

SERVES 4

Delima (pronounced d'lee-ma) is the Indonesian name for pomegranate. A ripe one when you open it has deep pink or ruby-colored seeds that are very juicy. Agar-agar (often shortened simply to agar) is extracted from various species of seaweed (*Eucheuma, Gracilaria, Gelidium*). It will gel even without refrigeration, so it is ideal for use in the tropics. It has no taste of its own. I have chosen here what is in my opinion the most delicious and finest-looking agar dish.

INGREDIENTS

2 tablespoons agar-agar strands, soaked in water	3 eggs
2 ripe pomegranates	1/2 cup coconut cream
4 tablespoons cold water	pinch salt
5 tablespoons sugar, divided	4 cups cold water

METHOD

■ Keep the agar-agar strands soaked in water while you are preparing the rest of the ingredients. To open the pomegranates, make a deep short slash in the middle of the fruit with a sharp knife, then with both hands press the fruit hard and it will break open completely. Now take out the seeds by hand, carefully, so you don't squeeze the juice out. Collect the seeds in a bowl. (Don't squeeze the juice with a lemon squeezer because the yellow membrane surrounding the seeds produces a bitter liquid.) The liquid from the membrane will leave a permanent brown stain on cloth; therefore, discard the membrane.

■ Set aside a few seeds for decoration and put the rest in a small saucepan. Add the water and 1 tablespoon of the sugar. Simmer for 2 minutes. Pass through a fine sieve lined with muslin or cheesecloth, then squeeze as much juice as you can into a bowl. Set aside to cool.

■ Break the eggs into a bowl and beat with a wire whisk until frothy. Add the coconut cream, whisk to mix, then add the salt and the remaining sugar. Heat this mixture, preferably in a double saucepan, stirring continuously, for about 4 minutes, or until the mixture is thick. This has now become the serikaya. Set aside.

METHOD

■ Drain and rinse the agar-agar strands. Put them in a saucepan with the water, simmer, stirring occasionally, until the agar-agar has dissolved. Strain the liquid into a measuring cup, then put half into the bowl with the pomegranate juice and the other half into the serikaya bowl. Stir the contents of each bowl vigorously with a wooden spoon.

■ Pour the pomegranate agar into a mold and chill for a few minutes while you continue stirring the serikaya. Take out the pomegranate agar from the refrigerator, pour the serikaya on top, and chill until needed.

Steamed Custard in Peaches or Nectarines

SANKHAYA

SERVES 6

"Sankhaya" is the Thai name for what in Indonesia is called "serikaya." The Thais and (I believe) the Laotians pour the sankhaya into a seeded but whole pumpkin, steam the pumpkin, and serve it cold, cut into slices. This is delicious, but it is equally good with peaches or nectarines, and much easier to make.

INGREDIENTS

6 peaches or nectarines	pinch salt
3 eggs	3/4 cup very thick coconut milk
6 tablespoons grated palm sugar	

METHOD

■ Halve the peaches or nectarines and remove the stones. Scoop out a little of the flesh.

■ In a bowl, beat the eggs lightly, and add the sugar, salt, and coconut milk. Stir until the sugar is dissolved.

■ Fill the peaches or nectarines three-quarters full with the custard and place them carefully in a baking dish. Steam for 10–15 minutes. Eat this dish cold.

Indonesian Cinnamon Layer Cake

LAPIS LEGIT

MAKES ONE 8- TO 9- INCH CAKE

In Indonesia, Lapis Legit is usually eaten at teatime. It also goes well with coffee, either in the middle of the morning or after dinner. It should be sliced very thin and cut into pieces about 2 inches long—it is very rich and the pieces must be small.

INGREDIENTS

1 pound unsalted butter	pinch salt
drop of vanilla	8 egg whites
1 cup sugar, divided	2 teaspoons ground nutmeg
16–19 egg yolks	4 teaspoons ground cinnamon
3 tablespoons half-and-half	1 teaspoon ground cloves
1/2 cup all-purpose flour	

METHOD

- In a bowl, beat the butter, vanilla, and half the sugar until creamy. In another bowl, beat the egg yolks with the rest of the sugar until creamy and thick. Beat these mixtures together and add the half-and-half. Sift the flour and salt into the bowl, and fold in carefully. Beat the egg whites until stiff and fold in.

- Divide this mixture between two bowls. Stir the spices into one of them, so that you have one bowl colored brown by the spices and the other cream-colored.

- Grease an 8- to 9-inch-square cake pan with a loose bottom. Heat the broiler to its maximum temperature (if using a broiler inside an oven, heat the oven to 275°F, then turn it off before turning the broiler on). Pour a layer of the cream batter, about 1/8-inch thick, over the bottom. Broil this for a few minutes until the batter has set firm. Take out, and pour on the same thickness of the spiced, brown batter. Broil this as before. Continue this process, with alternate layers of brown and cream-colored batter, until the batter is finished. (A good Lapis Legit will consist of 12–14 layers or more.) Bake the cake in a 300°F oven for 10 minutes.

- Remove the cake from the pan and cool on a wire rack.

- Lapis Legit will keep moist and fresh in a cake pan or in the refrigerator for a week, wrapped in aluminum foil. It can also be frozen.

Steamed Coconut Cups

PUTU MANIS

MAKES 10–12 CUPS

Traditionally Putu Manis is green. The green color comes from the juice extracted from a fragrant leaf called *daun pandan* (pandan or pandanus leaves). I like my Putu Manis white, so if you can't get the pandanus leaves, I suggest leaving them out rather than using food coloring.

The normal cup used looks like an individual rum baba mold, so when you take your putu out it has a hole in the middle. But I use a Chinese teacup without a handle, or a small ramekin.

To extract the juice from the pandanus leaves you need 4–5 leaves. Put these in a blender with 5 tablespoons water. Blend, then strain the juice.

One coconut will be sufficient for the quantities shown here. (See page 15 for notes on shelling coconuts and peeling off the brown skin.) Peel one half and grate the flesh; use the other half, unpeeled, to make the coconut milk.

INGREDIENTS

5 eggs	pinch salt
4 tablespoons sugar	2 tablespoons pandanus leaf juice (optional)
1/2 cup rice flour	
1/4 cup all-purpose flour	1/2 cup grated coconut flesh
1/2 cup thick coconut milk	

METHOD

■ In a bowl, beat the eggs and the sugar until thick and pale in color. Add the flours, continue beating while you slowly add the coconut milk, salt, and the pandanus leaf juice, if desired. Beat the batter for about 3 more minutes.

■ Heat some water in a steamer; when boiling put in 10–12 cups to warm for 2 minutes.

■ Divide the coconut evenly among the cups, pressing it in with a spoon. Then pour in the batter, the same amount for each cup. Steam for 10 minutes. Turn out the cakes as soon as the cups are cool enough to handle. Putu Manis are normally eaten cold at teatime.

Coconut Cups

KHANOM TUEY

SERVES 6–8

This is a Thai sweet, similar to the Indonesian Kue Bugis, which is wrapped in banana leaves for steaming. Khanom Tuey is made of ordinary rice flour topped with thick coconut cream and is steamed in cups—again, the small Chinese teacups without handles are the best for this.

INGREDIENTS

1/2 cup coconut cream	3 tablespoons tapioca flour
pinch salt	3/4 cup coconut cream
2 tablespoons rice flour	6 tablespoons brown sugar
1/2 cup rice flour	6 tablespoons cold water

METHOD

■ To make the topping, mix the coconut cream, salt, and rice flour in a bowl and set aside.

■ Sift the rice flour and tapioca flour together into a bowl. Pour the coconut cream, a little at a time, into the bowl containing the flours, kneading the flour with your hand. Knead for 2–3 minutes.

■ Put the sugar into a saucepan, heat until it melts, stir continuously for 1 minute, then add the water. Stir until the sugar is completely dissolved. Strain the syrup through a sieve into a bowl and let cool.

■ When cool, pour the syrup into the soft dough and mix well with a wooden spoon. Divide this batter among the cups, half-filling each cup. Steam in a double saucepan or steamer for 6 minutes. Add the topping to each cup and continue steaming for 2–3 minutes longer.

■ Serve warm or cold in the cup; eat with a small spoon.

Sago Pudding

GULA MELAKA

SERVES 6–8

In Indonesia we eat it as porridge for breakfast or as a snack at teatime. Gula melaka, (palm sugar) is a coconut sugar, available now in the West in most oriental shops, packed in a small plastic container. Shave or chop this with a knife, or grate it on a hand grater, before putting it into the dish you are cooking.

INGREDIENTS

1 cup sago	3 cups thick coconut milk
1 1/2 cups water, divided	pinch salt
1 cinnamon stick	1 cup gula melaka syrup, made from about 3/4 cup palm sugar
1/3 cup palm sugar	
1/2 cup water	

METHOD

■ Put the sago into a saucepan with 1 cup of the water and cinnamon; let it soak while the other ingredients are being prepared. Chop the palm sugar, then dissolve it over very low heat with the remaining water, and strain. Cook the sago by simmering it for about 3 minutes, stirring continuously. Add the coconut milk, salt, and sugar syrup, and continue stirring for 10–15 minutes, or until the mixture becomes thick. (To make the syrup, boil the gula melaka for a few minutes in 1 cup of water, stirring continuously. Then strain through a fine sieve.)

■ Discard the cinnamon, and pour into a large bowl or several small bowls. Chill until the mixture is firm. It can be turned out of its mold or served in the small bowls where it has set; or you can spoon it out onto a dish, with the gula melaka syrup poured over it.

ACCOMPANIMENTS AND RELISHES

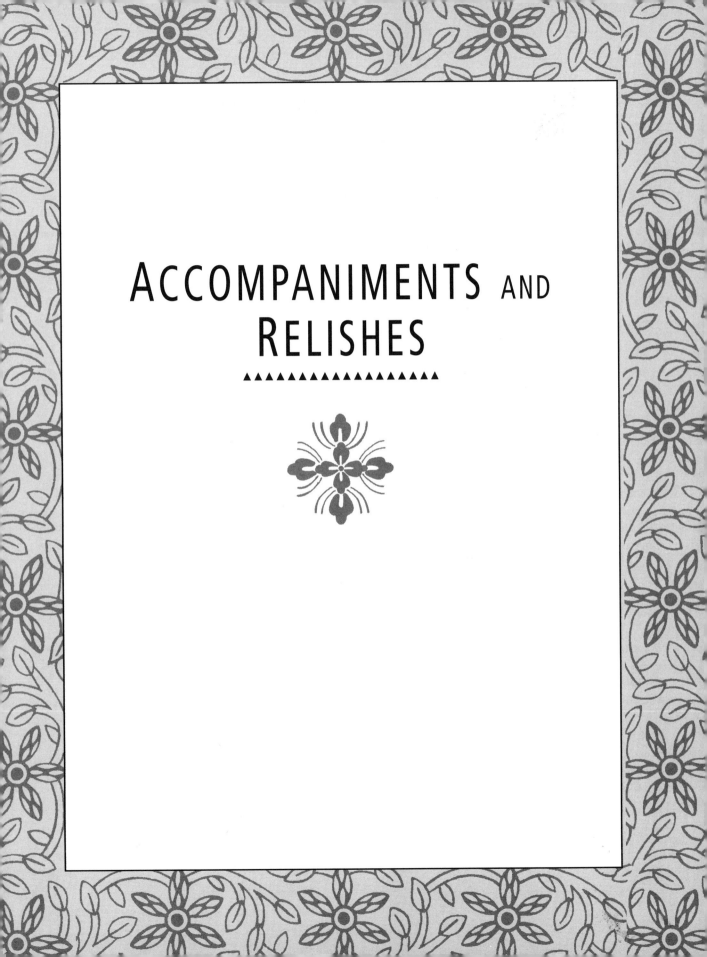

I suppose there ought to be a red triangle hoisted over this final section to warn the reader that some of these relishes are fairly hot—chile-hot, or pedas as we say in Indonesian. But they don't have to be uncomfortably hot; in fact, they need not be hot at all if you don't want them to be. What many people overlook is that chile peppers have a very characteristic strong, pungently smoky flavor, which is quite separate from their heat. This flavor is the real purpose of many of the preparations that are described here. I have greatly reduced the quantity of chile from what, in Indonesia and elsewhere, would be regarded as the barest minimum (except in the recipe for Sambal Ulek, which consists of little else but chile, so I could hardly cut it down).

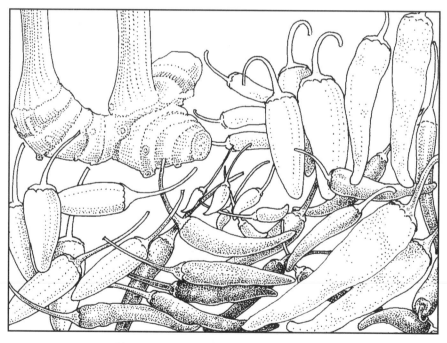

Chiles (different types and sizes), galingal

Crushed Red Chile with Salt

SAMBAL ULEK

MAKES 2 POUNDS

This is the basis of all the sambals that Indonesians use, either as a hot relish or for spicing a cooked dish. You can buy this ready-made in jars. It is sometimes labeled *sambal oelek* (oe being the old spelling for u). For any recipe that specifies red chiles to be blended together with other spices, you can use sambal ulek instead. So when you can get fresh red chiles from Chinese or Indian shops, buy a lot and preserve them as sambal ulek. This will save you from hunting around for chiles next time you need them. Sambal ulek can also be frozen. It will keep for about 2 weeks or more in an airtight jar stored in the refrigerator.

INGREDIENTS

2 pounds red chile, stalks removed	1 teaspoon sugar (optional)
1 tablespoon salt	2 tablespoons olive oil
1 tablespoon vinegar	4 tablespoons water

METHOD

- Put the chiles in a saucepan and cover with water. Simmer for 15 minutes. Drain and put in a blender with the salt, vinegar, and sugar, if desired. Add the oil and water, and blend until smooth. You may need to do this in batches.

- Store it in an airtight jar in the refrigerator, or freeze it.

Hot Chile Relish with Dried Anchovies

SAMBAL BUBUK TERI

I almost decided not to include this recipe just because the name translates so awkwardly into English. It's really delicious, though, sprinkled on fried rice or fried noodles. It is also good on an omelette, egg sandwich, or pizza. *Ikan teri* (or, as the Malaysians call them, *ikan bilis)* are sold in 1/2- or 1-pound packages with heads on. You need to remove the heads to make your sambal taste good.

INGREDIENTS

1/2 cup + 2 tablespoons sunflower oil	3 shallots, thinly sliced
1 pound dried anchovies, heads removed	3 cloves garlic, minced
3/4 pound pepper flakes	2 tablespoons sunflower oil

METHOD

■ Heat the 1/2 cup oil in a wok or frying pan and fry the dried anchovies in 2 or 3 batches, stirring continuously, for 4 minutes each time. Remove with a slotted spoon and drain in a colander lined with paper towels. Let cool, then pound in a mortar with a pestle until the anchovies are coarsely ground.

■ Discard the oil and wipe the wok or frying pan clean with a paper towel. Heat the 2 tablespoons oil, fry the pepper flakes together with the shallots and garlic, stirring continuously, for 2–3 minutes. Then add the anchovies, and stir for another minute. Remove to a plate lined with paper towels and let cool. Store it in an airtight container for up to 2 weeks.

Fried Shallots

GORENG BAWANG

MAKES 2 POUNDS

Both the Indonesians and the Thais use crispy fried shallots as a garnish on rice, dry-fried meat, and many other dishes. You can use onions instead of shallots if you wish; as they contain more water than shallots, it is a good idea to sprinkle them with flour before frying. However, I personally wouldn't bother to make my own fried onions. You can buy good ones in a specialty shop. Fried shallots are something different.

INGREDIENTS

| 2 pounds shallots, thinly sliced | 1 cup sunflower oil |

METHOD

■ Heat the oil in a wok until a sliver of shallot dropped into it sizzles immediately. Fry the shallots in 3 or 4 batches, stirring continuously, for 3–4 minutes, or until they are crisp and slightly brown. Remove with a slotted spoon and drain in a colander lined with paper towels. Let them cool before storing in an airtight container. They will keep fresh and crisp for about 1 week.

141

Crisp Fried Anchovies with Peanuts

GORENG TERI DAN KACANG

See Sambal Bubuk Teri on page 140 for an explanation of dried anchovies. You'll be more likely to find this relish in Malaysian restaurants than in Indonesian ones. At home, we serve fried peanuts and anchovies separately, but in London I go along with the Malaysians because dried anchovies are quite expensive and mixing them with the relatively cheap peanuts makes sense. They are also very good to serve with drinks.

INGREDIENTS

1/2 cup sunflower oil or peanut oil	1 pound dried anchovies, heads removed
1 pound peanuts	1/2 teaspoon cayenne (optional)

METHOD

■ In a wok or frying pan heat the oil and fry the peanuts in 3 batches, stirring continuously, for 4 minutes each time. Remove wth a slotted spoon and drain in a colander or on a plate lined with paper towels. Use the same oil to fry the dried anchovies in 3 batches, for 3–4 minutes each time. Drain in the same way. Allow to become cold, then mix well together and put in an airtight container. Add the cayenne, if desired, and shake well to mix. It will keep for up to 2 weeks.

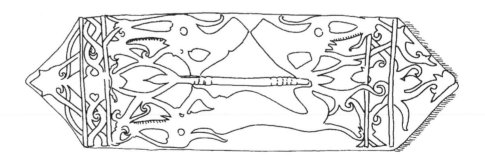

Peanut Sauce/Saté Sauce

SAMBAL KACANG/BUMBU SATÉ

INGREDIENTS

1/2 cup vegetable oil	1/2 teaspoon cayenne
1 cup raw peanuts	1/2 teaspoon brown sugar
2 cloves garlic, chopped	1 tablespoon dark soy sauce
4 shallots, chopped	2 cups water
1 1/2-inch piece shrimp paste	1 tablespoon tamarind water or juice of 1/2 lemon
salt to taste	

METHOD

■ This well-known peanut sauce for saté is not difficult to make. It really is not necessary to use crunchy peanut butter.

■ In a wok or frying pan heat the oil and fry the peanuts, stirring all the time, for 4 minutes. Remove with a slotted spoon and drain in a colander lined with paper towels. Leave to cool. When cool, pound or grind the peanuts into a fine powder, using a blender, coffee grinder, or pestle and mortar. Discard the oil except for 1 tablespoon.

■ Crush the garlic, shallots, and shrimp paste in a mortar with a little salt. Fry the mixture in the remaining oil for 1 minute. Add the cayenne, sugar, soy sauce, and water. Bring this mixture to a boil and stir in the ground peanuts. Simmer about 8 to 10 minutes, stirring occasionally, or until the sauce becomes thick. Add the tamarind water or lemon juice and more salt, if necessary.

■ When the sauce is cool, store it in a jar in the refrigerator. Reheat as required to use for saté or as a dip for crudités or other savory snacks. It will keep for up to 1 week in the refrigerator.

Tomato Sauce

SAMBAL TOMAT

Like all other sambals, Indonesian tomato sauce is usually chile-hot, but in this book, since I am suggesting it for general use, I make it quite mild. By all means add more chiles if you want to.

INGREDIENTS

2 tablespoons sunflower oil	1 cup water
4 shallots, sliced	1 pound tomatoes or canned tomatoes
1 1-inch piece ginger, minced	1 teaspoon salt
1 1/2-inch piece shrimp paste (optional)	1 teaspoon sugar
3 (or fewer) red chiles, seeded and chopped, or 1 teaspoon sambal ulek (page 139)	

METHOD

■ In a wok or small saucepan heat the oil and fry the shallots, ginger, and shrimp paste, if desired, mashing the shrimp paste with a wooden spoon and stirring continuously for 1–2 minutes. Add the chiles or sambal ulek, stir again for 1 minute, then add the water, tomatoes, salt, and sugar.

■ Simmer for 10 minutes or until the tomatoes are well cooked. Mash the tomatoes roughly with the wooden spoon. The sambal is now just as we would use it in Indonesia. However, if you want a smooth sauce, pass it through a sieve into another saucepan.

■ Adjust the seasoning and heat again for 1 minute if you want to serve the sauce hot, for instance to pour over the Tod Man Muh (page 73). This sauce can be served hot or cold as a dip.

Sweet and Sour Chile Sauce

NAM CHIM

This Thai sauce is widely available in bottles in most Asian shops, but it is quite easy to make. It is used as a dip for snacks or grilled fish, stuffed chicken wings, etc.

INGREDIENTS

1 pound red chiles, seeded and chopped	4 tablespoons grated palm sugar or granulated sugar
2 cloves garlic, chopped	6 tablespoons white malt vinegar
2 tablespoons water	2 teaspoons salt
2 tablespoons peanut oil or olive oil	1 cup water

METHOD

■ Put the chiles, garlic, water, and oil in a blender and blend until smooth. Put the remaining ingredients in a saucepan and add the chile paste. Bring to a boil and simmer for 30–40 minutes until reduced by half. Let cool before storing in a jar or bottle. This will keep fresh in the refrigerator for at least 2 weeks.

Soy Sauce with Chile

This sauce is particularly good for saté, especially for those who do not like peanut sauce. It is very easy to prepare. It's good as a dip for miniature spring rolls (page 30), as a light topping for fried noodles, or as a dip for crunchy raw carrots and celery.

INGREDIENTS

2–4 small chiles, seeded and minced	1 teaspoon olive oil (optional)
2 shallots, finely sliced	1 tablespoon light soy sauce
1 clove garlic, minced (optional)	1 tablespoon dark soy sauce
juice of 1 small lime or lemon	

METHOD

■ Mix all the ingredients in a bowl and put on the table for everybody to share; or serve in small individual bowls as a dip.

Prawn Crackers and Emping Crackers

KRUPUK UDANG DAN EMPING

Both these crackers are used to accompany food or as snacks to serve with drinks. They can be bought uncooked in many Asian shops. The Thais also make excellent prawn crackers. You can safely assume that emping are vegetarian crisps, since they are made of a nut called *melinjo*. Choose a package that still contains plenty of whole emping rather than one with too many broken pieces. They are quite brittle and get crushed easily.

METHOD

- To fry krupuk or emping you need a wok or a deep frying pan. The ideal temperature is 350°F. Fry the krupuk one at a time, rocking each one gently with a spatula as soon as it is in the hot oil. You need another tool to hold the rapidly expanding krupuk so that it comes out more or less flat. Let cool a little to make it crisp and delicious.

- Emping can be fried a handful at a time. Stir them continuously, and remove them from the oil with a large slotted spoon as soon as they have turned color a little—this will take about 20 seconds.

- Both krupuk and emping will keep crisp in airtight containers for at least 2 weeks.

BIBLIOGRAPHY

Jennifer Brennan, *Thai Cooking* (London: Jill Norman & Hobhouse, 1981).

Alan Davidson, *Southeast Asian Seafood* (Singapore: Federal Publications, 1977, and London: Macmillan, London, 1978).

Clifford Geertz, *Negara: The Theatre State in Nineteenth-Century Bali* (Princeton, NJ: Princeton University Press, 1980).

Clifford Geertz, *The Religion of Java* (The Free Press, 1960; reprinted by University of Chicago Press).

Elisabeth Lambert Ortiz, *Caribbean Cookery* (London: André Deutsch, 1975, and Penguin Books, 1977).

Sri Owen, *Indonesian Food and Cookery* (2nd ed.) (London: Prospect Books, 1986).

Mustika Rasa: Buku Masakan Indonesia (Jakarta: Departemen Pertanian, 1967).

William Shurtleff and Akiko Aoyagi, *The Book of Tempeh* (New York: Harper and Row, 1979).

Phia Sing, *Traditional Recipes of Laos* (London: Prospect Books, 1981).

M. L. Taw Kritakara and M. R. Pimsai Amranand, *Modern Thai Cooking* (Bangkok: Editions Duang Kamol, 1977).

The two books by Clifford Geertz are obviously not cookbooks; they contain some interesting background information about food cultivation, cooking, and eating in Bali and Java.

INDEX

Foreign recipe names are set in *italics*.
  Only major references are given for common
  ingredients.
  Indonesian c *is pronounced* ch *in* church.

OTHER COOKBOOKS BY THE CROSSING PRESS

Homestyle Cooking Series

Homestyle Mexican Cooking
By Lourdes Nichols
$16.95 • Paper • ISBN 0-89594-861-3

Homestyle Thai and Indonesian Cooking
By Sri Owen
$16.95 • Paper • ISBN 0-89594-859-1

Homestyle Italian Cooking
By Lori Carangelo
$16.95 • Paper • ISBN 0-89594-867-2

Global Cuisine

Global Grilling
Sizzling Recipes from Around the World
By Jay Solomon
$10.95 • Paper • ISBN 0-89594-666-1

Global Kitchen
*Meat and Vegetarian Recipes from Africa,
Asia and Latin America for Western Kitchens*
By Troth Wells
$16.95 • Paper • ISBN 0-89594-753-6

The World in Your Kitchen
*Vegetarian Recipes from Africa,
Asia and Latin America*
By Troth Wells
Foreword by Glenda Jackson
$16.95 • Paper • ISBN 0-89594-577-0

OTHER COOKBOOKS BY THE CROSSING PRESS

International Vegetarian Cooking
by Judy Ridgway
$14.95 • Paper • ISBN 0-89594-854-0

Island Cooking
Recipes from the Caribbean
By Dunstan Harris
$10.95 • Paper • ISBN 0-89594-400-6

Japanese Vegetarian Cooking
From Simple Soups to Sushi
By Patricia Richfield
$14.95 • Paper • ISBN 0-89594-805-2

Indian Cuisine

From Bengal to Punjab
The Cuisines of India
By Smita Chandra
$12.95 • Paper • ISBN 0-89594-509-6

The Spice Box
Vegetarian Indian Cookbook
By Manju Shivraj Singh
$12.95 • Paper • ISBN 0-89594-053-1

Taste of the Tropics
Traditional and Innovative Cooking from the Pacific and Caribbean
By Jay Solomon
$10.95 • Paper • ISBN 0-89594-533-9

Traveling Jamaica with Knife, Fork & Spoon
By Robb Walsh and Jay McCarthy
$16.95 • Paper • ISBN 0-89594-698-X

Identification of photographs following page 96:

To receive a current catalog from

The Crossing Press

please call toll-free,

800-777-1048.

Visit our Web site on the Internet at:

www.crossingpress.com

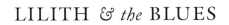

LILITH *& the* BLUES

"And thorns shall come up in her palaces,

nettles and brambles in the fortresses thereof:

and it shall be a habitation of dragons

and a court for owls."

☙ *Isaiah*

LILITH & *the* BLUES

Joe — There is much of love in this book, explicitly on p. 24, but elsewhere Too — Bill

POEMS BY

William Hollis

with photographs by Andrea Baldeck

William Hollis

HAWKHURST BOOKS

Poems Copyright © 2008 by William Hollis
Photographs Copyright © 2008 by Andrea Baldeck
ISBN 978-0-9748304-2-1
Hawkhurst Books, 6122 Butler Pike, Blue Bell, PA 19422
www.williamhollis.com

"Portrait of a Friend" appeared in *Shenandoah* (2007).
Sculpture on book jacket and page 9: *Lilith* by Arlene Love.
Some Blues were originally in *Scenes from an Old Album*
written and published for my parents on their 50th wedding anniversary (1977).

"I am sister to dragons and companion to owls.

My skin is black upon me and my bones are burned with heat.

My harp also is turned to mourning,

and my organ into the voice of them that weep."

∞ *Job*

CONTENTS

MOMENTS WITH LILITH

1.

She's there as I fall asleep in a chair
and my book falls shut and slips to the floor
with a slam, and I wake and call out, perhaps
with her name or with a moan of sorrow
or touch of laughter; but no one's there,
not even the inevitable she
I always thought would be close enough
to hear and respond with an owl's voice.

I'm caught somewhere between a cry
and a laugh, in the moment it takes to catch
my breath, in the moment it takes
to remember the book that slid away,
a moment to find that the sun is bright
and gold and falling beyond the window.

2.

I rise to open the door, but no door is there;
I reach to catch the door, but there isn't any door.
My hand abruptly closes on itself,
fingers against palm, with no weight of the door,
no holding back night or opening to light,
just a sudden shift of a world that jars me awake,
a sudden shift of dreams I'd almost had
that might have shown me what the answer is.

I reach to pull the door, but no door is there;
there isn't any door and my hand closes,
my fingers bite the palm and I wake
and wonder what it's all about, this life,
this moving in and out a door that may
be only a figment of the imagination.

3.

No? What is there to explain? I can only describe:
There is somewhere out there, in vast plains of space,
a group of identical women, all of whom look
like someone sculpted by a favorite, aging artist.
They all look down and around and fail to focus
until I come and stand very still just in front of one;
and if I'm not careful, she'll suddenly look up,
catch my eye, and hold hard to the twist of the moment.

If I should have to say something else, I'd simply say
that perhaps as we wander through inner freedoms,
we'll meet one of those wonderful figures,
and then go off in a different direction,
up and down another set of stars, out there,
somewhere out there, a long way away.

4.

What's her voice? What's the tone, the accent,
the burr in the voice I hear when I hear her voice —
Katie's voice, from the east coast of England,
elegant and touched by waves of the North Sea;
or the edgy, sharp and brittle voice of Debra,
twisted to pain by the Russian/Jewish diaspora,
a voice schooled in the Bronx with a decade in Tuscany?

If fathers of the tribe threw her out of Isaiah,
whether in elegant tones of King James or flat
earnest drawls of the Great Plains in an account
that makes sense in a dull, conditional way,
what am I supposed to hear when I hear owls
full of painful warnings and a cave of dragons
that whir an uproar of curses across the night?

5.

We let her fall until the wind
has caught her wings and brought her round,
and she settles on a sandy knoll,
a moment's rest, a time for us
to turn away and breathe relief.

Is she there long enough to wander
the palace Isaiah knew, out there
where dunes move slowly across earth
and horizons change and inevitably
the path drops into a crevasse?

Is it her ghost we hear now,
the lingering echo of her power?
We let her fall, but still she's here;
such power isn't so easily dropped.

6.

Distant cousins board their windows against Lilith
and if I didn't make something of that, she'd know
that I was ill.
             She knows I watched for hurricanes
when I was young, saw the force that pulled a tree
and thrust it through a neighbor's window; and all hell
broke loose; and all dogs barked and police arrived;
and I jumped up and down on the sofa by the window
so hard I peed in my pants to see what a force of awe
a temper like that might unleash.
                          The scream of wind
as it folds a garbage can around a grapefruit tree
is nothing compared to the voice that brings a curse
from god and wraps it all around a careless poet.

So here's to the namer of storms who remembers
the force of that woman when he wakes at night.

7.

I often awake to a sound of many bells
that, for a moment, I think are echoes of
her voice, bells that call from towers beyond
the woods, across fields where owls still hunt,
bells that call the hour in cities we know,
knowing the names of bells that mark the hour,
and not knowing, until recently, that she
will speak in tones of bells that wake us
in the night, in moments when I wake to hear
her voice, the pull of her voice, an ache she knows,
a cry she utters when lingering sun
goes down and she is left to fly among
towers, ringing bells and calling us
to remember her, to remember her voice.

8.

She carries a serpent in her arms
and strokes its head and holds it out
for us to see, a show and tell
that leaves the class confused and scared.
She's the only one like that,
beautiful and full of pain,
unwilling to play the game and fraught
with something the others never know.

I try to talk with her and feel
we might have a song to share,
might understand the pain
that pulls us from an empty dance;
but then one day she isn't there,
not even her name is called in class.

9.

I see her at the stove when I know
she should be flying with her owls.
Perhaps she'll look hard at the pot
and the dish will be ready to serve.
I wonder if Lilith stands at the stove
and stirs the broth of a chicken,
watching a bit of her own blood
enrich the pot and give it life.

I wonder if she sings for children,
sings in a low voice, hoarse
and edged with tears. Is it she
I wake at night and hear call,
in a voice that calls for me to rise, to come
and accept the hugs of what will be?

10.

The triple barking of Cerberus is still,
relentless wrappings of moon and stars
spin out to give sleep to the night.
Owls of Lilith settle and wait to see
what might come from fog that swirls at sea.

No child should wander on a night like this;
doors and windows should be closed and locked,
candles lit, and someone should play the flute,
play loudly as darkness pulls us close.
We should sing despite a heavy fog.

Heavy winds come, owls begin to cry,
candles flicker as winds rattle the window;
something sad and beautiful whispers
of failing growth in a garden's last breath.

LILITH IN THE FRONT HALL

1.

She slips from the house at night, mates with owls,
wakes the neighborhood, frightens a child
out looking for a stray cat; and it's she we expect
to encounter when we wake unexpectedly
and wander upper rooms, too tired to descend
to see if she's still high on her pedestal
where placed for a short time by force of love.

That's why the heavy gates are locked: she still
frightens, carries dismissive power, laughs
and rides high over anyone else. My daughters
find her uncomfortable, here at the entrance,
as if she were waiting for them when they visit;
yes, and others pause and look long,
caught beyond what they are willing to see.

Thousands of years ago, thorns grew with nettles
and brambles, dragons curled, and vultures circled,
every one with a mate, Isaiah wrote,
gathered over vast stones of emptiness;
while a great owl made her nest until her young
were gone, and she flew, a last time away —
a legend in pellets left in far gardens.

2.

It's Lilith, riding high on a saddle, her skin
ripped by the artist to reveal roughness, a swell
of our beleaguered world, who says it is
her preference for the top, to ride out years
while watched horizons rise and fall, as those
below rise and fall, breathing heavily,
unsure why they are panting for escape.

"Just hold," Lilith had said; "it won't be long."
And it wasn't. She was first, devoured apples
and argued with serpents who enjoy debate,
until the council of Jenna in 110 AD
wrote her out, gave all to Eve, while during
the diaspora, her ancestors rode rivers
and crossed mountains to join sea to sea.

No, she isn't Lilith until she meets
the snake, wings and head hiding in branches,
and climbs from childhood, mounts the world on a dare
no one can match, to desert places where
she pulls an image, an umbilical chord
from deep inside her gut and leaves us Lilith
circling these silent rooms where she still roams.

3.

Such rooms as this, here in a wooded suburb,
are stirred by arrogant liftings of her head;
and guests pause and find it difficult to move
when someone says, "Haven't you sometimes felt
that if your lover uttered one more denial,
your skin would dry and split with age, revealing
a splintering roughness you had never known?"

So Lilith spills her guts and the rest of us
mill around and slowly die, slowly
forget a time when we could work all day,
follow our own Lilith through desert places,
watch her tracks as they rise and fall through dark
crevasses where a desperate cry weaves
a dream we've never yet been able to escape.

She goes on, the artist who saw this Lilith,
who gave her birth, who leaves her here, alone
with older generations of pain we've known.
We all go on, more slowly, struggling on sand
to look back at rising shadows, to pause
and wonder if that's Lilith ahead, a shadow
that slips down a slope we've not yet found.

4.

If Lilith struts and Eve scurries to find
a way — "over here," she cries, "over there" —
where are we, in what dry, crumbling city?
It's been a hell of a lot longer than we
remember. Lilith with lifted chin, released
long ago from dark memories, struts
across this last stage where curtains descend.

Even Buddhas who cluster in other corners
show discomfort when they look at great thighs
that clutch with pelvic thrust and arrogance.
They're usually quiet, a shadow of serenity;
but when carried to another spot where they
might enjoy briefly blooming pots of orchids,
they almost laugh on a harried afternoon.

At times they disappear, slip into closed
annals, not seen for days; but Lilith is always
here, dominant, determined to be known.
She wasn't, but she is now, thanks to anger
her maker felt and used as fabrication:
"It's I," she says; "it's I." And so we nod
and glance at Lilith and know that she too smiles.

MANGROVE SWAMP

1.

Descending through a mangrove swamp,
bemused by possibilities of snakes,
we wonder why we'd had to leave the hill,
and its high, clear garden where lines
of space had stretched in all directions.

"They said there'd be a path around this muck;
but now I'm not so sure," she says
and tries to show a reassuring grin.
"They tell you what you want to hear,"
I say, and reach to touch her hand.

"Is that a sea beyond the palm?"
she says, and shies from thorns that rip our skin
and leave a smearing trail of blood.
We break through matings of twisted vines,
forget our fear, and rush for waves.

2.

A brief horizon seems much closer here,
the surf is high and loud and cool;
"It's worth it, after all," I say and splash
and stretch my naked body out
and feel the sand and grit I'd never known.

I watch her, thin and naked, stoop
to pull a shell that catches sun
and gleams like flesh in anticipation.
She turns to ask if we might pry it open,
if it might taste like an apple's flesh.

I wonder how it might have been if she
had been the one to be erased;
she doesn't know she was an afterthought
by those who grew afraid of Lilith,
thinking I needed one less intrusive.

3.

If she were here, I think we'd ride the sun,
even as it sinks down through the sea,
following demons of the dark.
But this is better, I tell myself, it must be:
we'll never climb that hill again.

The dark gathers a screech of circling owls,
rising high like angry surf;
and we're surrounded by rhythmic beats
of breaking waves and hissing fronds,
an echo of cries and sweep of wings.

"Please," she cries, "can we go home?"
I hold her close and try to warm her chills.
But when I look into her face,
I see the other one reflecting light.
"What was her name," I murmur, "her name?"

SPECIAL GUEST FOR A DRINK

Her house had washed away. The river rose
and rushed for the sea as if in vengeance,
wild horses in panic when a man draws near.
Vengeance or fear? In another world one might
have said a god was angry, giving threats
because she would not take her proper place,
because she demanded to know just why
he wanted another to take her place.

She's back now, for awhile, and comes for drinks
between rain squalls and a rainbow,
a whole half circle that slowly comes our way
until it vanishes and the wind dies down
and half a moon hangs just above her head
drenching her in melodious light;
and for a short while, if only for a while,
she smiles as if she's relaxed and calm.

"It's not so bad to wander. China last week,
where I'll soon return to a garden in Chang-an;
and there's a spot on the coast of Mexico
where dragons wait...." We laugh, refill her glass,
and push an argument or two to the edge
while wondering at those who take such matters hard,
who never pull back from an edge or leap to space
that opens wide and free of knowing the end.

Another rush of clouds swallows the moon
and darkness holds us close and there's a rumble
from the sea and silence as we sit and sip
our wine. An evening in the tropics,
an evening with one we think of as a friend,
until there comes a rush of dispossession
as if storms of time were rushing in; and then
she rises with laughter almost like a cry.

As rains come down we scatter for shelter
and find a candle for a little light;
but she is gone again, and it's a long while
before we hear, before her voice comes clear
for a moment, down a line from somewhere else:
"Thank you for the evening," she says. "It's rare
I have such time; but I'd like for you to know...;"
and our connection breaks with a brief burr of flame.

෧෨

OLD CAT GROWLS

She growls the way my old cat did when I approached
with words of greetings and a gesture that could become
the laughing hug I tried to give reluctant daughters.

She growls and stakes a moment's smile, almost convincing,
and turns as if she feels she's taken the game too far,
and hesitates as if there's one thing more to say.

I wait as I often did when the girls were young, so young,
and hold my breath and wonder if I should call aloud,
if I should forget my hesitation and laugh aloud.

She growls and curls into a small world that's warm,
protects, if only the rest of us will go away,
just let her be, just let her find her own way home.

I sigh and shrug and wonder how it gets this way,
remembering that I stepped on the old cat's tail when she
was young and left her calling through a night of pain.

As years went by, she spent her afternoons behind
the office door I never closed; I'd drop a greeting,
she'd growl, and I could almost swear she dropped a smile.

LOVELY DAY

I've had a lovely, quiet day for this and that,
listening mostly to piano music of Fauré,
reading Sunday papers, finding
nothing particularly interesting,
adding some books to the computer program,
rearranging some piles of music,
again trying the blues at the piano,
advising a daughter on color relationships,
picking okra and trying to decide on a recipe,
taking a comma out of a poem done last week,
adding a comma back to the same poem,
knowing that now the poem is finished,
suddenly realizing that a recent letter to Helene
of Troy N.Y. might make an interesting poem,
with lots of work, also realizing that Helen,
if not Helene, was herself a Lilith figure,
who swung her pain through early blues,
when still African and sung in cotton fields;
and now it's only three fifty-seven, which means,
since no one else is around to share a cup of tea,
that there's another seven hours to go,
which means that I had better get started,
which makes me wonder if I could do a poem
with the perfect syntax of a single sentence,
with the sentence structure of these lines,
perhaps for the *Letter Poems* volume,
which continues to grow and will probably
turn out to be the longest volume of them all,
since it still boils down to an I and a *you*,
as does it all when I play with words,
even if it's a lovely, quiet day and I'm alone.

PORTRAIT OF A FRIEND

She doesn't know she's Lilith; she's played an Eve
and learned to polish apples by the bushel.
"It's what I do," she says, and lowers her voice
to clear her throat and laugh and coax a smile
without a splash of real delight — her eyes
intrude for just a moment, revealing more
than she intended, almost splashing salt
across the room with a cry of "Please… please."

She's been a friend with whom I've never talked,
except at tea, across a table where lights
will flicker like fields of stars I used to see
across the night in a sky above the sea;
and now she reaches for my hand and sighs
and finally I think she'll speak her heart
and let that fire within her eye explode
with songs of dragons in a desert place.

"Tell me, would you really like to know?"
she says with just a hissing burr of voice;
"Would you really like, just once, to know it all?"
The room is closing in as silence falls
and even cicadas die and desiccate.
An Eve could go no further with that thought.
It takes a Lilith's anger to break the hold
propriety has placed upon the heart.

CAPTAIN BOB AND LILITH

Captain Bob was thinner than ever,
his bones gnarled and stretched with skin,
his flesh consumed, his joints wrapped;
"To keep me from slipping through drains,"
he said and tried to remember who we were —
if Andrea had taken his picture before,
just after that girl had arrived; "My friend,"
he said and grinned and showed his gums
and glanced toward the shack out back,
where we'd seen her before, out back,
frowning at intrusions, standing in shadows,
waiting, it seemed, for something else.

"For just awhile," he had said, back then;
"she wanders when the moon is full."
And, sure enough, we'd seen her there,
on windy dunes, when the moon was full,
trying to fly. Or maybe later she did,
up and over crushing waves, later,
when we'd wandered back to town
and saw Captain Bob wandering alone,
looking in darker corners of small streets
that were silent, except for hooting owls
phrasing a four-note melody,
a perfect theme for an old composer.

It's a melody, a rhythm I hear each time
I look into the dark or write of Lilith,
the half-mad girl with Captain Bob
who haunts the unpainted shack out back,
or the sleek Helen strolling the walls of Troy
wearing silk as wings to carry her home.
She's there still and Captain Bob
is a battered Paris, as Andrea tries to get
his picture for a book on mad poets
or wrathful Buddhas — as I try to see,
once more, the sheer intensity of Lilith
in mad hallucinations and rhythmic words.

HE'S GONE

1.

"He's gone," she says and holds a shell to the light
and murmurs, "It's not for sale; he bought it for me;
and now it holds my memory of him."

I glance at her in discomfort when the skull
of some raptor crumbles as I push it aside
to reach an eye of sea-worn green and gold.

"He won't be back; he left on the coldest day.
It's always that way: they leave when the house is cold,
when you're trying to find your way out of the dark."

2.

We'd never been this close to her; she'd hid
as if afraid, a fear of being seen
by strangers come to pull through piles of junk.

We'd seen her at the back of his peeling shack,
hiding her face, stumbling as if in anger,
if not in fear. "It's how she is," he whispered.

I put her in poems once or twice, with dragons
and owls, among images of Lilith,
with those who ride high above fallen truth.

3.

And she isn't even aging, not like the ones
who hide in dark corners of old bookshops
and fade with the covers of old poems.

The ones who startle with a sudden offer
to help you find what you might want, laughing
because they know you haven't seen them watch.

She's not exactly young and may be pregnant
by a spirit restless among boxes of shells
and shelves of books that carry a dragon name.

4.

"The dragon sings; the tiger cries," I whisper
before a worn and imitated drawing —
something else, she says, that's not for sale.

Something else he'd bought and hung here, just
for her; something that will stay until
she goes to find him — somewhere else, she says.

But dragons will always sing, I say, just listen;
perhaps he left a song for you to follow
beyond the growling laughter of the street.

5.

"I've placed my loneliness among the shells.
He'll know. That's why he left these many things
for me — there has to be a place for me."

The voice of a dragon that frightens so many
lurks like a song in the upper reaches of the room.
"It calls me," she says and hands me small black shells.

"I have a dragon's name; I'll fly," she says —
and smiles and turns away, and leaves us to hear
the wind as it blows through a set of rusty chimes.

DAUGHTER LILITH

Can one ever speak with a level head of daughters?
Are there daughters who ever speak with a level head?
Do all fathers want to replace Lilith with an Eve?
Even mothers who have themselves been mad creators
may wish to protect daughters from that painful fate.
Of course, this may only dramatize limitations
of the metaphor; real life is more complicated.
Maybe there are eight Liliths standing on the terrace,
waiting, each one different, and indifferent too;
eight seemingly calm images that reflect madness.

We tried to share a tale with laughter, but it faded
into an intensity of memories that spilled across the table
and dominated twilight. "They would not dare," she said;
"They would not dare to question my instructions.
And if they did…." There was a darkness in her eye
as storm clouds gathered over a great stone house
and forces of a hurricane moved closer, and the sea
washed ashore. I could feel threats gather, a chill fall.
Scholars of the past might have erased the moment
and left the tale unfinished, a bit mysterious.

By the time she left, pulling a gold and black truck,
so mammoth it had to be parked at LuLu Temple,
down the road and up on a hill, deserted and dark,
I wondered who would die first, who go mad at stumbling
with words or flesh and high-lifting flashing legs and mane.
She has decided garlics are a devil's poison,
that butter, grains, and bacon are the only breakfast,
that neither her mother nor her sister should visit,
that her father could be ignored except for advice
about color or punctuation for an essay.

Could a father have let her fall until the wind caught
her wings and brought her around and she settled down
on a grassy knoll, a moment's rest, a time for us
to turn and breathe relief? Could it have made a difference?
Lilith must soar with whatever storm is blowing in.
Let it blow, whatever pain rains down, whatever fear.
We've held on long enough; now we must let go, turn loose
and let her find her way back through erasures of time,
back into her own world. Maybe then we'll laugh again,
maybe then we'll see clarity and a morning sun.

☙

NO DEAD END

Every time I think we're almost there,
alarms go off and lights begin to blink;
and, damn, we say, just look at that: It's great;
it's just the sort of thing that she would do.

She's into that, has driven half way there
and turned around and gone some other way.
Oh sure, like us, she's often left herself
hanging over the ledge and breathing hard.

Of course, she's just like that: she'll slip away
and end nose down in a dry river bed;
but then she's out and trotting through a field,
shouting to look at that, just look at that.

Now here we sit and wait to see what's next.
The lights go out, the sky's gone dark; but, look,
the stars are bright and show a way out there,
the kind of way we never thought we'd take.

BITS AND PIECES VIA PASCAL

"Bits and Pieces" could be another title for a book
                 on the creative process,
which might also become, as this poem may,
                 a philosophical approach.... To what?
Well, to life, I guess; or to a study of Pascal. The latter,
                 I think; for come to think of it —
and I haven't done so for many a year — it's Pascal
                 I return to more than any other writer,
except maybe Yeats or myself; and years ago I gave some bits
                 and pieces of a summer to a far-fetched idea
of doing an edition of Pascal that discarded all positive
                 references. (Actually that last period
is a bit of a joke since his positives are numerous and only
                 those sweet on God would end in the pile.)

If I'd had any luck with responses to my poetry, I'd have
                 encouraged a graduate student
(a very beautiful, very bright redhead, like Lilith)
                 to write an analysis of the poems
from a de-deified Pascalianism (with a whole section
                 on a strangely Russian couple, artists,
who exist in bits and pieces through the poems). In fact,
                 one could go back to ones written
under the whish of pine trees and tickle of palm fronds
                 on a sandy beach in Florida before the invasion,
when sharks swam close and greeted us, almost nose to nose,
                 and we simply splashed loudly
and drove them away, with no help
                 from life guards or even a parent.

It was decades before one of the pieces from those days,
                 an offer by an old friend
to play around in a Lilithian way that I didn't know,
                 at least in the chill of gulf waters,
came to mind when I heard he died and no one was willing
                 to say just why he died.
It was one of the bits one didn't talk about in old days,
                 down there with too-many preachers

who, it turned out, had their own pile of bits and pieces
             to deal with and couldn't
and so shot themselves to avoid clucking tongues;
             oh yes, and there was another
who ended in jail, and another who ran away with a boy
             from the choir, and one shot by his wife.

My, my... as mother used to say: that's a neat little pile
             of pebbles. I just wish I could spread them
all out; though I guess I have: Old friends get copies of bits
             and pieces before anyone else
and see stones before and after they've been through
             the smoothing machine. That's it:
Photographs or paintings or poems are polished stones
             displayed in woven baskets
after they've been through the tumbling machine
             of our enterprising selves.
I actually have a literal one, never used, on a high shelf
             in the barn; for why, I ask myself,
would I need one? I spend most days turning bits and pieces,
             trying to polish them.

Sometimes bits and pieces get in the way and bumped
             and left with jagged edges
where Pascal might be caught by Lilith. Maybe he was
             and that's why his own bits and pieces
tumble: "What a novelty, what a portent, what a chaos,
             what a contradiction, what a prodigy,"
he might have said, and did. And here we are,
             caught in the relentless job of trying
to tame Lilith or even to sing the blues with a touch
             of defiant anguish,
or to make that photograph or that painting give a holler
             in the field, to cry against darkness —
trying to say we may be in bits and pieces,
             but we're still defiant.

DON'T PRETEND

I can't sleep, can't pretend she's not around,
got to find words to let me hear her say,
"As a moon passes through another cycle,
honey, I'm here, waiting; and I laugh
and dance as you retreat.
I strip and offer the richness of skin.
See, here it is, waiting for you
while you think you can pretend to sleep."

I think there's nothing more
until the voice cries out again,
"You don't hear, you never hear,
you turn away and pretend to sleep.
But I know: I watch the trembling in your back.
There's no escape.
I'm here, circling above you.
Listen — don't pretend with me."

They never told me about her when I was a kid,
never taught me to duck beneath blankets.
And now she says, "You'll never get away
as I whisper in your ear and bring chills,
like now, right there, down the spine."
And for a moment I feel her nail
scrape my skin, and then I hear
her wings pull through a window.

Somewhere there's laughter,
forced and faint as from cotton fields.
"You still pretend," her voice drifts back,
"that I'm not here, that you're free to sleep
or scratch lamentable words.
But I'm here, with an owl that circles the house,
with a memory of dragons.
Listen — don't pretend with me."

MISTER PRESIDENT AND LILITH

Because he said the sky was blue, I hurried outside
to watch a piling of clouds, high and dark and purple.
He said we should not fear, for God was on our side;
and I could only remember rumblings of Isaiah
about lying on a bed that's much too short for comfort.

When he said we should all join hands and sing chords
of perfect harmony, I had to laugh, as Homer did
when gods and men continued to color earth with blood.
He said we'd dance our pain away and grill a pig
and call the neighbors in to shed a city of solemnities.

It would be much easier if I could believe Isaiah
about a world at rest and quiet, or even about
a golden city of Babylon, how it might be as we'll be,
he keeps telling us, if only we bomb the rest
of this damned world and get them to pray with us.

So lambs get fed to the lion and words of Isaiah ring
with rhythms of a dragon who dwells in a pleasant palace,
and I can't help thinking that if he spoke a poet's tongue
from a furnace of affliction, we might listen and hope
to find our own damned way through the wilderness.

PURSUED BY THE PAST

Steps are hot; a scholar's hand has pushed
dusty age from the random stone she climbs,
leaving me to wait and wonder why
I feel deprived, indifferent to an age
so clearly part of what I'd dreamt as a child.

After lunch, an ordinary occurrence,
cool and quiet, as if at home,
we leave the others, sleepy in the shade,
and climb through woods where stones were left
to tumble with a tilting of the earth.

We slip and slide and, in a shade of limbs
that have cracked a temple's wall, pause to hear
a wind that whispers through the afternoon
for just the two of us, the only ones
around, the only ones to hear the cry.

And then an echo in ancient rooms,
a scratching from the past, another world…,
and stones crumble beneath our touch
in a splutter of time, before a wind
returns and ravaged limbs stir in anger.

Leaves go still as memory cries
for us to remember what was here before
a ship dropped sail and tilted to the sand
and two worlds faced a deep crevasse.
Even the shifting of the earth is still.

We can't remember how long it is, an hour,
a painful lifetime's memory, until
a toss of trees in a sudden storm brings a voice
that calls for our return, the bus must leave,
an evening's party at the inn is next.

ANOTHER STRANGER

There was a moment I looked up
and thought, *It's she.* I was sure. "You,"
I said, "It's really you?" and paused
as she grumbled in her drink, laughed
without humor, without a smile,
just the laugh, harsh, without pity.

We had encountered each other
from time to time without pleasure:
on a bridge that swayed with the wind
above a gorge of shattered rock;
in a searing moment when light
ripped apart the lingering dark.

And always she laughed with no smile,
as if she were poling a raft
through fog and lingering silence
as my hands twisted in the ropes,
holding to a sad bitter end
even if it was not yet here.

I never heard her name. She came
when least expected and ordered
a drink and sat at the far end
of the room, pulling at her hair,
until suddenly she was gone
with only laughter lingering.

BLOOD IN THE SNOW

1.

It all started with a smear of blood in snow,
red, brighter than lipstick she wears;
a bird's head and feet, a feather or two,
though the body's gone, devoured by one larger
and more insistent than enchanted Merlin.

It's beautifully done, this photograph she sends,
caught with an ordinary digital camera
and quickly manipulated so a smear of blood
can be shared with casual friends in other places
where snow never provides a ground for work.

By now it's melted, the blood's gone, except
for remnants in the mud below her window;
and she has probably begun a poem
about those of us to whom she sends that print,
a warning smear of blood that hints at words.

2.

It started years ago, when Merlin stood
in snow and awe of the lady down by the lake
and watched her hair as it caught the setting sun
and gleamed like blood flowing toward his hands,
though he paid for that with the rest of a stricken life.

In fact, on this dark afternoon, what's left
of this bird has made me wonder if it was the owl
of Lilith who circled in and took his breath
and left him stammering through all time to come,
stammering like a poet who has lost his words.

So Merlin must wait in a tower while an owl
circles outside his window and a smear of sun
falls across remnants of snow; and somewhere
she waits, wondering if her photographic
colors will hold in a manipulation of madness.

A CALL

There is a snuffling on the line, a sigh,
and silence, during which the kettle begins
to simmer. "Are you there?" she sighs again.
There is nothing to say. It has been too long.
Tea leaves fill the room with odors
as distracting as a draft from a window
that should have been repaired last summer.

"You never listen when I need to talk,"
she says again, as every year or so she does,
calling to cry at another broken heart,
loneliness she's found at the top of a mountain.
The tea is ready, though too hot for the tongue.
"What are you doing?" she says and pauses
as if she can smell the afternoon kitchen.

"Is anyone there? Are you alone?" she says
and waits as if to be offered a cup. With sugar,
it always was, a lot of sugar and milk.
She doesn't want a response; she never did;
it's enough to murmur and sip at the tea
and wait. It helps to have the mug in hand,
a little bitter and smelling of the delta.

The snuffling continues, an occasional bark
to make sure that someone is listening,
that somewhere through a darkening afternoon
her words are touching even a reluctant ear.
The tea is cooling rapidly, has lost its taste;
the draft seems sharper than before, colder;
the window must be reglazed as soon as possible.

YEARLY VISIT

From the moment she arrives until she leaves
three hours later — or is it all of a week —
she sucks air from rooms and leaves us gasping
(reminding me of teen-age daughters in anguish).
It seems so real, perhaps a grand gesture
from Russian steppes, from cold and darkness.

"I can not eat," she says, "I never eat
until the sun has set and darkness lingers."
And then she fills herself with second helpings,
handfuls of chocolate cookies from the oven,
as mid-day sun reflects from snow and ice
and warms the table she fills with anger and tears.

"They're only from a damaged eye," she says;
"I have not wept since they said he'd not return,
and that was fifty years ago or more.
I was a child who only wanted to paint,
who never remembered how old I was; I heard
and pulled black paint across a sheet of paper."

She has brought her latest catalogue, with prices,
for she knows how interested we will be,
though she has already fired the gallery
for their inadequacy on her behalf.
"I shall have to shift my enterprises," she says;
"perhaps I'll sell myself." She does not smile.

DIVA'S ROLE

It isn't often I get to hear you sing;
you play a role in Rome or with your ex;
and I'm left here to write these lines alone,
amused by the new brunette who still can smile,
who doesn't have to flaunt a tight little ass
as she takes an order for beer and burger
and glances at the notes I've jotted here,
these notes I try to ignore because I know
you'll never see them even if you get
the book I send, again, knowing it's vain,
an empty gesture, no way to attract attention,
not from you, whatever role you play.

I heard your voice while driving past the fair,
the big one on the edge of town, with cars
and horses waiting for a run, and traffic
so heavy in all directions I never heard
whether it was you or just another diva
spilling her passions for the world to hear
she got the role that everyone wanted
and now everything else can be kicked aside,
discarded, the way you discard lovers and me,
though that, you said, was a mistake: "Never,"
you said, and laughed; and I had to admit a poet
with a diva was a little hard to imagine.

What role are you playing now? It's getting late,
and I find myself watching the new brunette
at the bar treat me like a grandfatherly sort.
She throws me a wink as the guy to my right leans
and tries to make arrangements for after work.
Have you taken a new lover this season? Do you sing?
You haven't made the pages of the Times?
There's another role in that, the fallen one,
the one who lost her way, who only had
a grazing brush with fame, who wouldn't care
that she lingers in memory, here and there,
if only in the notes I make during lunch.

GREEN PAINTING

May I just say your green painting becomes more intense?
May I add that it has become a semi-tropical woodland
full of swamp oaks and Spanish moss? Should I add
the scene is a scene of my boyhood in south Georgia
and carries life memories that I wake and see
in the middle of the night, without rising or finding a light,
without going into that other room where it hangs, waiting,
always waiting for me to enter, to pause, to move closer?

Should I also add that if the makers of Tolkien films
had used it as the land through which hobbits wander,
those films would not have been so dull, might linger
as the book lingers, as we hope to linger after adventures?
May I add that I miss our rare encounters, verbal or actual,
and hope that you gaze into a Greek sea and perhaps
hear an ancient lyre and a sad murmur of Greek verse
that may have been chanted by a man named Homer?

May I presume to say that, even as we miss you, as we do,
we work to avoid interruptions in our own green world?
And may I ask you to keep an eye out for Lilith, who has
taken over much of my current poetry, at least what doesn't
rise as white blues from those heavy oak forests along
a coast where I wandered as a child and again now?
May I, my friend, take these words, this form of a letter
and cast them among scattered greens of that woodland?

SHE NEVER SMILES

She never smiles, though she might laugh
with a touch of bitterness or fear.
We watch her wander streets and pause
alone for a cup of coffee and a nod
to acquaintances who pass in a rush.

She's always dressed with care, sitting
across the terrace, as I try to figure out
what might be a clue, a gesture
at which we'd think, "Ah, ha, that's it,"
in the slowness with which she rises.

But she doesn't, rise slowly that is, she rises
suddenly and with grace, glances at her watch,
and slips away from tables and tourists
and disappears in the narrow dark streets;
and for a week or two she'll not appear.

We'll not remember; we'll not care:
there're plenty of others to catch as they flee
from scrutiny and slip over a narrow bridge
until we see them reading a newspaper at the bar,
self-contained and for a moment indifferent.

And then one morning we see her cross
the square as we sit with a friend and watch...,
well, watch whatever there might be to see.
"Oh yes," she says, the friend who knows it all.
"She'll never accept an invitation. I've tried."

But why does she never smile? I finally ask,
to silence and a sigh. And, if not then,
another time, I get an answer, evasive
and confused, that makes me blush a bit
and lose the smile I usually wear.

It's just for the words, another encounter,
I say, though no one listens, some words
to push out at the mystery of humans,
to put together in another rhythmic dance;
it's just for the words. I wouldn't hurt a fly.

She still doesn't smile, though I've nodded
and smiled when we pass in the park.
And I had thrown away the notes I'd made,
at least I'd put them in a file, until now,
when I see her pause at the crest of a bridge.

She's been hurting for a very long time;
perhaps she's at the end of patience.
Others have leapt before her and disappeared;
but she moves on, without smiling,
headed for another afternoon of loneliness.

And I'm left here, trying to fit words
into a pattern and suddenly feel
that it's a little late to stop now,
though I'll stop at the bar for a drink
and make notes about why she never smiles.

PANIC FOUND IN A LOVE LETTER

She often panics and writes with tales of a guy
from Alaska who holds her hand and helps repair
a big beast of a printer that drives her to cookies
full of enough chocolate to drive out memories
that wake her in the night, when she picks a book
and finds a quotation just, she says, for me:
"Our lives are rivers that flow into the sea
of Death" — comfort for early hours of the night.

And then last night she sends several notes
in a row, as if, while out flying with dragons,
she finds the guy who holds her hands has taken
a bus cross town to a South Street jazz club
to blow his horn with lingerers and has called
to say the jam's so great, the crowd's so good
he's going to stay for another set or two,
when it's already late for an old man like him.

She knows it's a bit of a stretch when the singer's
a hefty blonde who purrs when she says 'please'.
So how can a man resist...; what's a body
to do? "My own cat purrs," she says, "when he says
'oh, please,' and I melt and share my ice cream cone."
And this from a woman who flies, I thought, with Lilith,
who places on her computer screen quotations
about paths that flow into the sea of Death.

HELEN TRIED IT LIKE LILITH

Helen tried it another way and ran away
with a good-looking hunk who wasn't very bright;
that's why she's a Lilith no matter what dictionaries say.

And Homer and I, with Virgil and many others,
get hung in her story and try not to forget
the little guy, according to some, she settled with.

So here we are trying to explain Helen or Lilith,
for she's still wandering through generations,
sometimes with black, sometimes with red hair.

It's a little like the inside of a creative hut:
a gorgeous hunk of something that doesn't work,
a hunger for the perfect resolution of…. Of what?

A recipe, the paint that spreads across a ground,
the movement of a body loaded with music
or balances of color, dark and light, and shapes?

The passion that led her to stalk the walls —
remember? — made Homer wonder if Hector noticed,
makes me wonder if she'd slash his eyes.

Was it he or some other guy who pushed his luck
and got lost in the maelstrom of life, a storm
that stirs imagination, with a lust to give it form?

That's all it is. Not much. Except a passion
for words and rhythms they experience
in an effort to show us who's Helen or that Lilith.

BAROQUE PASTA

On a rapid slide down hill, we hear melodies,
baroque ensembles playing without terror
of knowing where it will end, a crest or crevasse.

The strings play Vivaldi as if he is a playground
where children climb or slide to mud piles, splashing
and laughing and driving parents to distraction.

We sit beside the fire and listen for an hour,
no television or telephone, just sounds
of strings weaving their way to a resolution.

Not even laughter on BBC can top
that twitching in my spine, the anticipation
in my groin. It's like suppressed laughter

that brings a gleam to the dark eye of a woman
I've only seen on the other side of the bar,
not even aware, perhaps, that I am watching.

But it is only the cello of a baroque ensemble
playing Vivaldi. Or is it Frescobaldi?
(Yes, it's saner when I can make these hasty notes

scratched across odd bookmarks or stickies
yellow and oily from pasta now ready for supper
with a splash of tomato sauce and cheese and words.)

MAVERICK

The house is crazy right now,
but you have not been forgotten;
yesterday I promised to write
in the afternoon or midmorning today;
and you wrote back a note
that saw a poem where no poem was meant.
Maybe that's a clue:
Good poems come unexpectedly
to a body that moves with verbal rhythms.

I had not known, had not seen
possibilities for a poem in those groans,
even as a test for continued endurance:
after all, she got off to encounters
early yesterday above the city
and then, late yesterday, to a distant valley
from where she'll return tomorrow
by dark, perhaps, if trade winds hold;
meanwhile, trees come down, slowly, one by one.

It isn't really bad, just a testing —
for a vista opens dramatically
in each place a tree comes down;
and a new Chinese cabinet arrives
and looks great; and the rehanging
of a wall here and a corner there works well;
and my doctor says, "You know, you're really
in pretty good shape for an old sot."
Well, she didn't add 'old sot'; I did.

And right now, the house is calm —
perhaps because everyone has left —
and the massage woman, a red-headed Lilith
will arrive in an hour to rub out the care;

if, that is, she doesn't decide to bring
her haunting owls, which she's want to do,
according to Isaiah I Book 34.
And right now is the right moment
to find words that send virtual hugs to a friend.

And should I add that I'm mighty glad
you've tackled the mavericks? Who better?
Just you. Even if I've not seen yours,
I know them: I've lived with mavericks
all my life...; or rather, I've been one,
living with Liliths while fathers of the tribe
pound the desk and mother Eves
click their tongues in exasperation,
"Poor little Maverick; he's really lost."

෨

BLUE EYES OF BODICEA

She does not blink, her eyes, large and blue,
hold across the table, will not set loose,
as if she told herself she had to stare —
for if she stared she would not have to say
just what it was she didn't want to say.

She does not blink, she opens wide her eyes,
with a brighter blue, a shining pair of shields,
the sort great armies of Bodicea wear
in tramps across rocky ledges at night,
Lilithian forces on the move with dragons.

Against the moon they move like dark dreams
and push for freedom from the past, she says,
a past you'll never know, she says, as blue
from her eyes forces me to lower my head.

RIVER'S POEM

1.

Should I tell you that just this afternoon, one week
since we saw you last, we retreated to a café
around the corner to eat and talk and talked
a great deal about the earth, the sea, and you?

And now, having started in quest of a poem for you,
shall I wonder what you would do if suddenly moved
to record a quest, suspecting you would hoist sail
and take the next current in our direction — or away?

2.

Would it bother you to know your mashed avocado
tanning oil is now widely discussed at dinner tables,
where aging Liliths with disappointed smiles
express lascivious interest in a body so tanned?

Would you be interested in a new gathering
of wanderers, where, I confess, they now gather
in fifty sonnets with Eve no longer twenty-three,
though you'll find her, envious, among Liliths?

3.

Will you recognize yourself when you are there
in bits and pieces, often with bits of Lilith
thrown in? Will you understand, after such palaver,
why this version flows darker to the sea?

Will you or Eve understand why words get darker
though one's will sails forward with pleasure?
Will you see, even in notes, a push to harbor
for which I quest in a quest that pushes me?

4.

Does it make sense that even if one has little new
to say one needs to exchange words and does so
even as words tack as images do and should
before a photograph or painting is ready to be shared?

Do you see where the quest has slipped, bucking shoals,
watching for a clear channel in spite of a flippant flow
of words, without a grounded doubt or question
that an artist-psychologist such as you will understand?

5.

Do you know how well you flow, with tides
that carry Lilith to freedom and pain — do you know how far
you've got her under your skin and mastered tides
on an endless river from which you chose your name?

Will you mind if a letter, starting out to touch base,
turns into a poem with a push of tides that prod
and flow with your name and blustery spirit
as "River's Poem", certainly as a river that flows onward?

STONE AND LILITH

1.

There's a beautiful peripatetic in the house,
brought from there to here and, once here,
moved from here to there; at first, he was
in the dining room, jealous of all books

occupying the best places; and, right now,
he rests (or, if unable to rest, sits restlessly)
on a Korean weaving, surrounded by orchids
in bright shades of the sky; he's on a small table

created by a major American furniture maker
in the central room of the house and within
the protective warmth of Lilith riding in her saddle
high there, right there above him in a way

I would think would satisfy; but in a night
of stillness, he moans in discontented rumbles.

2.

Today I shall probably move him — Stone
is his name — to the music room within shadows
of a dragon rock (or rather the rock
where my dragons live within the shadow

of a large, black piano), though that might be
intimidating to such a sensitive creature;
but if he doesn't calm down, there will be
another move into a nimbus thrown

by a pair of prints from a grand lady, which ought
to shock him into a certain respect — ought to,
but the problem is that, having emerged gloriously
beautiful from earth through natural forces,

he dismisses as sullied by the hand of woman
any competitive glory of human creativity.

3.

Well, I did — moved him when headed to bed
and again when headed to the piano for Bach,
and again, several times — until finally
I gave in and placed Stone, alone and on

a piece of unpolished wood from a tree
that had fallen in a storm, a bit of the natural,
in a corner where one either saw him
and the slab of rotting walnut or saw nothing,

nothing of the distractions he so resented,
nothing of the objects human passion
has made in anxiety to leave something
behind, something to comfort the heart,

the comfort he could not give since blown
from deep earth in a hot pouring of rocks.

4.

Too bad, I think, when I pause to admire
the glitter of his prisms turned to the wall,
Lilith might have understood his loneliness;
she might have recognized another

rejected by the earth, spat forth in fire;
she might have picked him up in the night
and stroked him, not minding the blood
left on her fingers, knowing the impatience,

anger, even fear he could never express,
except by catching reflections of the slightest fire,
a light somewhere outside the window
and across fields where Lilith herself,

late at night, circles with her owls,
like a dragon, like the dragons we all have.

NINE BY NINE SMILES

1.

Until the book fell open and spilled
her name across the desk and its mess,
I had forgotten what a smile is,

what a sudden force it can become,
unexpected until suddenly
there again, out of all memory,

from the back dark corner of the shelf
where it has spent years gathering dust,
open now, full of her sentences.

2.

For a moment I am astonished
to see three small golden birds settle
in shallow water left between stones;

like domesticated suns that fall
free of larger rules, free to splash wings,
as rare creatures that help me with smiles —

so I smile at my astonishment,
forget the tasks I had set myself,
and decide that it's enough to smile.

3.

The eye can never decide just what
it sees, just what it needs in moments
when smiles slip and the darkening eye

becomes more pain that will push drama
to other sides of a crowded stage
where girls linger to see if we need

help to take another role, the role
we have to play until dark curtains
fall for one last time without applause.

4.

Would she have smiled at the fall of dust,
at the fall of that small yellow bird;
would she have looked up and perhaps smiled

to see me struggle with her fallen
memory, with sentences I'd loved
so long ago I'd forgotten them,

forgotten how they had moved my heart,
forgotten how they could heal my heart
if she tried to smile through memories?

5.

I pick up the book, afraid to read
and almost close it with a dark sigh,
until words catch my eye and twist hard

with memories that still linger there
wondering what had happened to her
after this unmeasurable time,

after long tangles of fallen youth,
expectations of another world,
smiles with a crumbling of memory.

TRIBUTE FOR A LILITH

1.

Someone must tell the tale, give it shape, form
to be carried by all who know what happened.
In no way have her ashes blown with the wind;
and I suspect, from examples I've read and words
I've heard, pain I've watched at the edge of an eye,
that not even time can be dismissive of her story.

There's something strong and defiant about her:
She's Lilith, erased from books of Moses and Isaiah
by church fathers, by male establishments afraid
of strong females. But she's determined to survive
and spend nights with owls and hoots of laughter
and circle the moon with dragons and tears.

She struggles to survive loss of a son over an edge,
to survive loss of a family, being left by the world
with pain and laughter. That's her achievement.
The rest of us are mere observers at the edge
of a stage watching dancers attempt not to cry
as they pull too little in an effort to keep moving.

As an old poet, I hung out in court with Xue Tao
after she retired from efforts to survive the sex trade;
she built herself a poem-chanting tower by the river
where many poets visited and brought gifts,
brief poems on small squares of beautiful paper
that have faded now, even as her story remains.

Someone from the shadow must tell the story,
vigorously and with passion and without judgment.
Who will do so now? Who will be the artist
who will, instead of sounding like a judge,
say to hell with the judge and take hold of the heart
with all those verbal skills that prod and flourish?

2.

Surely, I think, after we return from the island
of escape, surely there has come a moment
when chimes remind us of what else is missing
in the world: another set of sentences that move
like music and carry the rhythm of her dance,
the stare that reminds us of her dragons.

And then, last week, I read of a new book
about Madame Pellier who danced and stripped
herself into the center of life in the twenties;
and then, on Sunday, a review of a new book
on another Lilith who had a history and death
from a similar time as muse and celebrant of life.

Surely, I think, how lucky any of us are to be
at the center of a maelstrom, to see it all again,
to have the tale that should be told, of a woman
with power and individuality. Who else would play
scrabble with a knife leaning against the board?
Who else can illuminate the toughness of the world?

A new club opens in New York, in an old fire house —
the best club, we're told, since The Blue Angel closed —
where guests pay too much for shower curtains
to surround a table. Maybe they could be energized
with words. You know, the sort of words with which
you and I fill a page, then two hundred more.

A Lilith should not go unknown, not now, not after
thousands of years, not after women have been shoved
in closets, if not behind a stove. I've watched
the ones who broke away, who stripped on a table
for all to see, who refused to tolerate the shit;
they're the ones whose history should be recorded.

FAMILY TREE

No Liliths survive in my family.
If one began to emerge during a moment
of potential freedom, she would be wrapped up
and rushed to a special hospital in Atlanta
and given drugs and loving care until she died.
And several died. One was really crazy,
they said, and made my mother weep.
"There was never one like her," she said,
"a magical musician with so much to live for,"
forgetting an aunt who wore a knife on her belt
and strung a wild pig to a swamp oak
and slit its throat and ripped out the innards
and served the meat in a bloody sauce,
which was enough to bring the elder males
to a meeting of the minds and another reservation
for life at that special hospital in Atlanta.

And now a gutsier generation has come along,
you'd think we'd learned a thing or two;
but elders of the tribe still sit in council
with prayers or curses, even a blow or two,
and cross her name from the family's proper list.
And though a few of us have learned
that Lilith's hell is a hell of a lot better
than Eve's, for whatever it might be a woman
might do, the elders still turn their backs and vote
to delay the action until they've had a chance
to set us straight. And I'm left in a small room
making notes about the great flight of Lilith
across soaring lines of Isaiah, though few know
that it is she, flying with owls and dragons
through desert places of the night, free and high
with the wind at her back and wide horizons ahead.

ANOTHER WAY

Are you sure it's the way you say and not another way?
You used to respond with anger or delight and dare
an argument, response like a tumbling of storm clouds
that would meet above one of the seas
that separate us and drown any distant voice.

There's always another way, you know, over there
across that desert where brigands sing or lie in wait,
armed with tumults of dust bound to leave us gagging;
or out there, down a river that races to the sea
where surf can still remind us of human fragility.

We used to break a trail through anger and confusion;
we used to follow an ill-defined path through fear;
we used to lose ourselves in the density of passion;
and now we find this camping place on a wide ledge
and seem reluctant to disturb monotony.

Perhaps we'll find that waiting isn't as bad as we thought.
Remember when impatience drove us to the edge
and we didn't hesitate to push beyond;
remember when we shouted at the moon to grin
and keep on falling through skeletons of trees?

You drew an angry breath and said it would never end,
we'd have to draw a line and dare the other to cross.
And here we are on a ledge above the ordinary,
like raptors waiting for another chance to soar,
waiting for the right set of words to clear the air.

Are you sure there's not another way? Just look:
the sky is full of colors that clash and thrill like anger;
lightning can bring that tree lumbering to its knees.
Perhaps the transport can wait; perhaps we'll stay right here
and watch light fade across the way we could have gone.

WORDS ON WANDERING

I think of you and how we were before they took
my name away, when we stared at the moon
as it ceased to grin, was large and luminous
and kept roosters awake and feral dogs restless.
Now I spend my nights in flight like a blue heron
over coastal shorelines and shimmering lagoons.

I've just returned from a flight across these hills
behind the house where I watched torrential rain
batter this very window, before first light,
here where other worlds demand a flush of care,
not owls or dragons, but cats and restless pups,
until rain stops and light seems full of possibilities.

Then with Orinoco, that flowing pup, who's not
yet learned to pay attention, I wander out on foot,
a little grounded by light, but well amused
by him and awed by shadows cast across the hills,
no way dark enough for flight, even when,
as we near the end of our walk home, we're slowed

by two wild stallions who follow us to the gate
and ignore me as they sniff goodbye to the pup,
unlike the jolly dragon who often circles the moon
a second time for me to enjoy a storm that passes
without a breath of wind, but low dark clouds
and sounds so magnified I feel as if I'll always

have power that night and moon give me for a name.
And then I hear the buzz of a fishing boat as it leaves
the pier in the village, so I must rush up the hill
to watch it find its way between *los dos cayos*,
great stones from ancient days, and reluctant sun,
lost in the east where sea has again gone dark.

Suddenly hundreds of butterflies, great flutterings
of tiny blues followed by large ones, orange and black,
sweep by like rare dreams and settle on trees;
and there beyond them a swarm of dragonflies
circle the heads of girls who play flutes,
golden in the possible light, and just for me.

(found in a letter from Colleen)

෴

WILD PAINTER

Now I shall be able to envision her at work —
both she and the work I've now seen,
as somewhere behind my eyeballs, her hand
reaches to test what it is I've really seen.
I tell myself to be still and watch how marks
mark the page in a crazy fall through space,
though I'm the crazy here, watching Matisse
or her there, unaware of what I've seen.

I shall continue to ignore judgment,
will just enjoy the liturgy of achievement,
for it's a long, long road to wherever we go,
so I'll just watch as she passes with piles
I just caught a brief glance of, yes, paintings
of herself who may end in a book with Liliths.

MELDA

Her smile is suddenly there, a smirk at the window
of the jeep. "I want ice," she says; "bring me ice."
And with a grimace half way between threat and hug
she turns away, grabs her barrow and returns
to a hot afternoon of filling road holes with pebbles.

We quickly drive on with a nervous glance back
at what seems a dragon stationed along the route home,
a dark dragon with sweat dropping from her eyes.
All afternoon I wonder if she is there, circling
and full of intruding threats and possibilities.

After a restless night, an early morning, a list
of errands and supplies for island explorations,
we pack a cooler with the last ice from the house
and set out, knowing that somewhere along the road
we'll face the power of this dragon's gutturals.

And, yes, as we slow at a curve, she is there.
"I want ice," she says; "I want...." And before the smirk
is fully there, I thrust the great bag of ice her way
and hold my breath as she pauses to look at it,
to look at me and lift a piece of ice and laugh.

It's a real laugh now, spreading around broken edges
of her face, bludgeoned nose, furrowed brow
that suggests the great swinging face
in old paintings of the dragon who lived with Lilith —
real laughter, shared, our eyes touching across ice.

We hear a little of her past, survival on the streets,
the shade she shares with homeless children,
the anger she struts at annual parades, when ladies
turn away and shake their heads in disapproval;
yet all she wants is a little ice... and maybe a smile.

She has the sharpest knife on the island, one
that cuts through anything, including the hardest ice;
but she's a friend who wears hope on a ragged shirt
above a swollen belly: "RESPECT" it says in faded letters;
"RESPECT" in hope bright as the smile she shares.

AT THE EXXON

I forgot to mention a poem that happened at the local
Exxon, yesterday, when poems happened at every turn,
and it felt as if I were in a movie, though, actually,
the prelude or preface, or whatever it might be titled,
happened the night before when Deming called after 10
to read her story, her letter, or whatever it was.

I listened, heard and felt it with total attention, as usual,
though it was late for a phone call — but that's Deming,
who depends on my total attention and immersion,
for that's how I am — and she tells a wonderful story
about getting lost, trying to visit someone
in the suburban confusion of our neighborhood.

It was a letter, or it was a story, actually two in one;
and I felt only two jarring words in the five pages
she read — but visualized a different form
with each sentence, each thought a separate line,
as someone might do a poem; but she disagreed,
and I, for that's how I am, didn't press my view.

The main thing is, it's a cliff-hanger, it really is,
all the way through, my story, and beautiful too,
that I'll call 'At The Exxon' or something that will hint
at complexities of life this far out of town
where many of us have spent much of life getting lost
and trying to find ourselves once again, as you know.

That's why I needed to wake up this morning
and turn that call from Deming into a poem or story,
even though a meddling fool to whom I told the story
took my perfectly good account and like some editor
turned it into a poem, though I'm quite happy to say
he doesn't know what really happened at the Exxon.

(found in a letter from Helene)

BROTHER

I want to hug him as if he were a brother,
only I've not hugged my brother in seventy years;
I want to love him even when he snarls,
dismissive of me, the world. Hurt, embarrassed?
I'm never sure. I read his poems that seem
to ache for a tough guy stance: screw you, he says,
or him or her, the whole damned thing, he says,
he seems to say. But I never believe him,
not when he snarls at the waitress who splashes
his wine or me for asking out loud about the pain.

I want to give him a hug and urge him to talk,
to call, to write; but he only snarls, it's all right,
that's just the way it is; and if he drops a hint
to which I murmur, so that's it, he explodes
with denials of what he'd said before, of what
he'd written a year ago, a decade. I never said it,
he says, never said a word; besides, it's not true,
I didn't do it, never; it was she; they did it; okay,
it's okay; it's just a phrase in a poem or the book,
a translation after all, something from the past.

I return to his poems and enjoy them once again,
puzzled, elated, wondering why he throws us off,
wondering why he'll sign a brief note with love
and disappear into whatever world he's found,
out there, somewhere else that none can share.
Or is it that? Perhaps it's just the empty bucket
I keep under my own desk for discards, peelings
and wilted leaves, nothing more, the crap that's left
after a day I've spent here at the top of the house,
wondering just why he can't accept a friendly hug.

NEW MOON AND OLD TALE

A new moon, heavy, sinks toward the horizon
like a primitive boat full of potentiality
before it slips down the far slope of a mountain
into a sea already dark and unchartable, a heavy ship
like those on distant islands, seen on crumbling walls
or ancient manuscripts, shaped like a cradle for a night
or two in the west and gone before we sleep, dreaming
of brilliant glittering ships like one Odysseus took west,
one last time away, toward other worlds, away
from all the obligations they said he had at home.

Not even poets have told us where he landed then,
somewhere further west than anyone else had been,
perhaps out there where Lilith wanders with owls,
beyond worlds even Isaiah could have known
in descriptions of empty air where she and her dragons,
or perhaps a pair of feral dogs, roll with thunder.
We have climbed the mountain, climbed to the very top
and seen a golden boat as it touches a bright horizon,
reflected, magnified, until suddenly it is gone,
the sea is dark, storm clouds and sky are gone.

AGING DOWAGER

Apologizing for writing about her tasks
for daily survival and possibilities
that dangle from the hinges of an ordinary life,
she sends a sketch of what might follow after
interior matters. "You know," she says,
"after what must be done; and then," she says,
"you'll see, words will spread across sheets
faster than an iron across a pillow case."

She's what? Eighty or maybe more — maybe;
but you'd never know when words roll out.
They're full of piss and vinegar, as we used
to say, in deliberate attempts to upset mothers.
And now, older than a grandmother, she's heard
it all, said it all and doesn't give a shit,
just wants to find a pathway through the day;
you know, something that will let her stray.

And stray she does, or so it seems, in words
that skim across a painful morning, hinting
at other lives she lived when she was young,
after her rabbi called her in for a lecture
and told her she'd never fit in, never,
he said; if she insisted on questioning
everything her father had to say,
she might as well go wander on her own.

She wandered and settled in; she changed
her name a couple of times, and disappeared
and reappeared. We'd see her at a gallery;
we'd read a brief account and wonder when
the book would be at Fox's, slipping from
the shelves, and certainly reviewed with praise.
"It'll happen," she says: "the world comes round
and shadows fall, but I'll put it all together."

WHO IS THE AGING DOWAGER?

For a few moments I can't remember where a poem lurks,
hiding in what cluster of manuscripts; but then I look it up
    and say,
"Of course, it's Lilith; she should have known this." The Dowager
is actually an amalgam of an aging grace, to some extent, and
    a graceful contessa
from beyond the Veneto, a little like Iris Origo — but only a bit;
and a shrink in escape from Chicago on a tropical island,
using only a first name, and an old Helen friend who keeps
    pushing words into age.

But without a doubt (or without much), there's a gesture or two
    from you,
my dear, before you, or do I mean she, flew out to join owls for
    a circle or two
before dawn; though it's still Lilith, which is where poetry differs
from photography — for this poem is made from seven
    potentialities,
and maybe many more that I know of, but won't say,
or many more that I've not thought of until this moment
of wondering who she is and from where she might have come.

WRATHFUL BUDDHA

1.

She says the Buddha is compassionate;
and, yes, I've seen him smile, and written so,
in poems from yesterday or decades ago;
but not until I finished a work on Lilith
during a Wagnerian opera, last week,
did I realize a demonic image I've known
is wrathful Buddha, wide-eyed and grim.

She says it's a shame others have not found
demonic powers like this, a leering sort —
have not kept a Lilith to scare us shitless
and leave us longing for a world that never was,
the one my mother said was waiting for kids
like us, if we'd just mind our *Ps and Qs*
(though we never really believed a word she said).

Her mother had it right, she says; "It's dark
out there and likely darker before the end,
she said, and would not smile and rubbed her wrist
and said the city streets were not for me.
She's right," she says, "for gutters are full of trash
that drain through dark places beneath the piers
and stink like restless boys with itchy hands."

2.

But Buddha is compassionate, I say;
he used to sit beneath a tree and watch
the rising moon, as your brother did, you said;
"Though it never got him anyplace," she says.
"He's dead with all the others." The tides pull back
into a sea where creatures of the dark
laugh at what we thought we'd have by now.

And so you made a wrathful Lilith, I say,
like Buddha from a high mountain cave.
Perhaps the world's become a heap of fear.
You said your mother had it right, I say. "She had;
she'd seen it all before." Too bad our mothers
never met, I say, they might have seasoned
pots with something more digestible than fear.

"The time will fast approach," she says; of course,
I say, just watch blue clouds that rise from swamps
and watch that necklace of grinning skulls he wears
like dead heads hung across your dining room.
"She had such a touch of beauty," she says;
"and, my, how she rode high above us all, and leered."
I know, I say, as tears confuse her laughter.

3.

This Buddha's like a dragon in the rock, I say,
and stirs fear I woke with just the other day.
("It's maybe good to have that fear," she says.)
Do you remember? We were much younger then.
You wore those floppy hats and flashed a match
like a dragon's fire; and all the guys stood back
in awe, with just a little lust thrown in.

"And now the Buddha's rock is in your house,"
she says, "just there beside the black piano."
And sometimes in the night, I say, it rings a note,
one clear and perfect note, as if the Buddha
were testing for a tuning of the strings.
Sometimes we have to stumble just a bit
before we find a path around the stones.

Sometimes the Buddha snarls to remind us
that a lovely little melody from Brahms
may just begin a darker mood. That's all, I say,
that's all it is, a darker mood than known
when I was small and thought it all a game
to play for ladies at their luncheon clubs;
while now, in darker rooms, I play for just myself.

4.

"You know, so much of what we've said is shit,"
she says. It's easier to show it off in bronze:
that little pile of bronze that catches at the light
is just a monument to turds geese have left
across the lower field. In time, it feeds the turf;
and then you come and sigh at such rich green
and wonder how we make it so beautiful.

"My mother never would have liked the words.
'How gross', she'd say." And maybe that's why
there's a wrathful Buddha, a Lilith for revenge;
someone's got to see we need a spade to shovel it.
Perhaps that's Lilith making out with Buddha,
strutting there on a high rock of the mountain,
carefully drawn by a bemused Tibetan painter.

"Lilith always liked to ride on top," she says;
"that's why I put her high in saddle, whatever
Isaiah might have said about vultures who mate."
And can't you see, I say, it's much the same:
the wrathful Buddha grows angry at the world,
sees the horror and cries like Mr. Kurtz...;
and we're left with dusty objects for a collection.

TELLING TALES

It's a pleasure to receive again an English poem,
to find a clarity of verse still here;
and it's a pleasure to see her recent book
and a familiar portrait and say to myself,
"By all means, that's one splendid book and a woman
about whom stories must be true."

But I must admit the only tales I hear these days
are those I tell myself; and I do tell tales,
tell tall tales, many of them, about her and others
I've known, and new ones who pop up regularly,
as they and I wander with restlessness
and hope and a share of laughter and a tear or two.

It's never too late to have encounters, never too late
to say to myself, just look at that one, over there,
who smears a rotten avocado over her skin,
enough to make a saddle for Lilith at the full moon;
or look at him, peering over the bar, predatory
for seventy years, still a raptor under the moon.

It's not a joke: I've seen her restlessly pace
high walls of Troy, wondering when,
wondering if, watching distant horizons of the sea
to see if he'll come again, from over there,
sometime thrashing through a clatter of the sea,
"Looking for me," I hear her say, "just for me."

SILENCE

1.

There's more silence than I ever thought possible —
if it wasn't my brother grumbling in sleep, the cats
were fighting over which should have the window ledge
under a great black walnut where taunting owls
called down, perhaps suspecting that one of the cats
was Lilith preparing to come forth in the dark
and take her place among prurient possibilities.

And there were sexually eager nights when a mattress
creaked louder than a platform where dancers bounced
and the cry of a dragon echoed through the house,
calling for a little freedom from necessities,
a little freedom from regular beats of the line
that got the poem started, breaking the beat,
leaving images to veer and maybe even fall.

2.

I mean it's been a lifetime of noisy interloping —
the cries when I was born, apparently in pain,
and later a little anger at indifference by adults
who wouldn't take the time to share a hug
or verse I longed to hear once more before I slept;
and later still it was the rising of the voice
in well-phrased pacings of a fatuous argument.

And if the house went quiet, as it seldom did,
there I would be, banging on keys, pulling Bach
from neatly bound volumes, a little worn and dusty now,
and spilling him across drafts from an open window,
filling the upper rooms of the house, until I heard
a voice that asked if it had to be played so loud,
if the kid couldn't wait until everyone was gone.

3.

Not even churches held to that illusive silence:
If Miss Clayre was not shaking rafters with soprano
acrobatics, then two old friends of my father snorted
to startled jumbles when poked by their wives;
or the preacher, in a full range of bass-note warnings,
would drive me to the writing of angry words
on empty spaces in that sweaty morning's program.

Even when faith became a casual joke, except
as hinted at by Camus in a lecture to the monks,
I'd fill a room with rich rising sounds of Isaiah
as I discovered that he spun the tale of Lilith,
as did Job in a heavier fall of words: "I am brother
to dragons, and companion to owls," he said,
for we are "born unto trouble, as sparks fly upward."

4.

Just that word — silence, silential or silentious,
silentiaries — is pushed on to silentium altum....
But if I go to silenus, I'm back into the woods
with a braying ass, a satyr, back to the cheers
and boos of afternoon crowds, back to the traffic
that, if it stalls, becomes an explosive finale
with all windows down, voices rising in anger.

We can't put silence into words: words are full
of sound. Put them together and the rhythms
make us want to move, to strut a bit, to dance.
With words, a friend gives life to the loss of a poem
I had sent with love to show him what was going on.
I read them aloud in front of the computer screen
and feel them, those words, his or mine, echo.

5.

We tried, we thought we were coming close
as gardens were planted thick enough to hide traffic,
and heavy stone walls with closed windows hushed wind
and the brush of leaves; and at night I'd wake
and wonder where the world had gone.
Am I deaf, I thought? But it wasn't that.
Death, even if dust, is likely to be full of silence.

We went to the edge of a cliff over the sea, where,
even at the top of a mountain, even on a still afternoon,
breath would form a beat, a poem would begin once more.
Silence is just the passage between one sound
and another, the moment marked by sibilants
when a heavy push of wind slams a shutter and you turn
and laugh and admit we might as well listen to Bach.

6.

No, these are the sounds to hold to, to push aside
whatever silence might close us off. Of course there's more
than when I was young, when everything was possible,
except silence, or so it seems — except for all those
other things we wanted to add, fortune or fame,
a variety of Liliths to explore during endless afternoons,
new sounds at the piano, songs to astonish.

Silence may be just a moment of rest between joy
of this and disappointment in that, a cello that echoes
in dreams, the discipline that helps us move
from a focus here to an immersion there, a pause
that helps me to see the need of another beat,
right here, before the end, to make a balance,
to wonder if there will be, after this, a brief silence.

LILITH BLUES

Her name was Lilith and she lived in a shack
beyond cotton fields where trains rush by.
In the middle of the night, when trains rush by
her cot would rock like a train through the night;

     and she would cry, "Oh my, oh my,"
     as the late night train came rushin' by.

Her name was Lilith and she lived in a shack
where we'd ride high in that dry little shack.
Yes, her name was Lilith and she lived by the tracks;
for a while she did, if only for a while;

     and she would cry, "Oh my, oh my,"
     as late night trains came rushin' by.

Her name was Lilith and she lived in the shack
that burnt on the night my gal ran away
and left me cryin', yes, left me cryin'
as I lay on the cot while a train took the way;

     and I cried out loud, "Oh my, oh my,"
     and a late night train came rushin' by.

Her name was Lilith and she lived in a shack
that burnt all night after a fire was started,
and she cried and laughed as a fire reflected
on the bed that rocked as a train went past;

     and still she cried, "Oh my, oh my,"
     as a late night train went rushin' by.

Her name was Lilith and she lived by the track
and laughed and sang, "She's gone, she's gone
on the track that stretches beyond the shack."
And the bed shook harder as the night came on;

> and she cried and cried, "Oh my, oh my,"
> as a late night train came rushin' by.

Her name was Lilith and she lived by the track;
but I'm so afraid I was drunk that night
that I try to forget we was ridin' high
and laughin' until I was blown out of sight;

> as she cried and cried, "Oh my, oh my,"
> and a late night train went rushin' by.

Her name was Lilith and she took the train
and disappeared way down the track;
Now I'm a little mad and full of sighs
and growin' old and tryin' to remember

> how she sighed and cried, "Oh my, oh my."
> as the late night train ran off the track.

MINNIE SANG OF A PROMISED LAND

I.

She sat on the porch and sang to herself,
she sat on a porch at the back of the house
and sang to herself of Jordan and a promised land;
she sat on the porch all latticed in white and black
and strung a sack of beans and sang to herself
           of Jordan and a promised land.

While Roscoe and I lay with old Hound in clay
under steps of the porch at the back of the house
and listened to Minnie as she sang of Jordan and a promised
land that lay beyond silence and June bugs and soft laments,
as she sang with soft laments in her own sweet voice
           of Jordan and a promised land.

Nobody knows the trouble we caused with rotten figs
and peach stone and stick; nobody knows the joy of days,
when Roscoe and I lay with old Hound in dust of clay
and dreamt of chariots and fire and listened to Minnie sing
of thunder and home and raise her voice high to sing
           of thunder and home and a promised land.

We lay in clay and dreamt of rivers of fire and thunder,
and listened to Minnie string her beans and continue to sing
of rivers that rose on toes and slapped an enemy down,
rose and slapped an enemy down to mud that ran to the sea;
and her voice continued to sing of a fire from the Lord,
           to sing of Jordan and a promised land.

2.

In the flight of a bee from grass to tree, Minnie saw ghosts
and sang of those ghosts that wandered the woods
out back of the house where a bee would flee
for woods where wandered ghosts that she had seen
at night when the moon was low, and now she sang
                of ghosts that wandered the woods.

And she sang of an owl that lived in the barn
when the moon was pale and low and the bat and mouse
were silent; and if we looked, she sang, we'd see them
in the eye of a fox that glared all night, a fox that glared
in the room we shared at night, and shivered in fear
                of ghosts that wandered even there.

So Minnie sang of afternoons that always were,
while all through buzzing hills, men slept in shade
of pine and brush. She'd drop the song to an almost whisper
that afternoons were always, and all through hills
men slept like dust before streams where ghosts wandered,
                where even in sun ghosts wandered.

And all through afternoons, she sang and caused us to shiver,
caused Roscoe and me to shiver as her voice dropped low;
all afternoon the fox would gather a glare of light
in glass of his glittering eye, and all that night we'd see
the light while we listened to hear him move,
                while we'd fear to see him move.

3.

So Roscoe and me, we lay in clay as her voice trailed off,
and tried not to laugh, tried to stay quiet, tried to wait
until she woke; and maybe we slept and maybe not,
maybe we dreamt of ghosts she had seen,
maybe we slept as we lay in the dust and maybe we dreamt
            as her voice trailed off.

Then Minnie would wake and cry and start from sleep
and cry, "Oh my, oh my", and push at her chair
and snap the beans that covered her lap with green,
snap the beans and cry, "Oh my," as we giggled beneath
the porch and punched each other and tried to stay quiet
            as her voice trailed back to sleep.

And we would yawn, for it had been too long already,
and we'd pull the tail of old Hound for a sudden bark,
we'd pull his tail for a bark to make Minnie jump,
to make her jump and drop beans and scold with a tongue
that rumbled with thunder before she tried to return to sleep,
            to a sleep that flitted with ghosts.

But old Hound was tired of the game and bayed,
bayed long and high as if that fox in the bedroom were real,
he bayed 'til Minnie fussed and sent us off, somewhere else,
and off we'd run; though we'd pause to hear her sing,
we'd hear the voice we loved as she sang of river Jordan,
            as she sang of Jordan and a promised land.

WATCHED POT

I watch to see if there could be
                 a mystery,
a secret life that's shoved aside
                 for the hours she cooks,
leaning over steaming pots,
                 her skin in a sweat.

Perhaps the secret's hiding there,
                 simmering in the pot...,
that's all, ingredients she found
                 the night he left,
ran out and never returned, leaving
                 her dark and broody.

I didn't know until much later
                 her name is Tara,
the wrathful one, mother of Buddha,
                 a female Buddha;
until one night, seated near the stove,
                 I heard her sing.

She sang the blues for a guy who left,
                 who took the train
to Memphis and never came back, never,
                 gone forever.
"Forever," she whispered to the pot,
                 "he's gone forever."

She sang like Lilith and spit in the pot,
                 and called her owls
who circled down from the crumbling rocks
                 and sang her songs
in cries that left me full of fear
                 my skin in a sweat.

WHITE BLUES

I ain't black and can't sing the blues;
I lack what you have if you're truly black.

I loved dat boy and he was black
and hung in a tree 'til he was dead.

I loved dat woman, old as a skeleton,
who lay on a bed and bless'd us all.

I loved Kitty, black and mother of all,
it was she who took such care of us all.

    Oh no, I ain't black
    and can't sing the blues,
    except in my soul,
    except in my soul.

I ain't black and can't sing those blues I heard
as workers climbed a hill to the field.

They climbed with mules and hope for tomorrow
and came back down at night, still singing.

It was Minnie who hugged me when I hurt;
it was Roscoe who taught me to listen for whispers

that tell what the world is all about,
those whispers from ladies in the drowsy heat.

    Oh no, I ain't black
    and can't sing the blues,
    except in my soul,
    except in my soul.

It was Kitty who lifted me to the sun
and said 'you's all my sons' and it was so.

I can't play blues or sing rhythms of pain;
I can't tell ya how to push through the day.

I got white skin that's terribly thin;
but, inside, I'm black like a bucket of coal.

It's midnight when I dream — and dark —
and the dream it happens every night.

   Oh no, I ain't black
   and can't sing the blues,
   except in my soul,
   except in my soul.

There ain't any music to go with this,
except in my head, except in my head.

There ain't any music, 'cept in memory,
as I carry on to my own old age.

And if I ain't black, I'm like that mule,
breathin' hard as I climb the hill.

Every day I climb the hill
and then, in the dark, come down again.

   Oh no, I ain't black
   and can't sing the blues,
   except in my soul,
   except in my soul.

NO RIGHT TO THE BLUES

I thought that I could sing the blues,
could make the passion count;
I thought I had a right to the blues
because they echoed pain I'd heard.

But I was on another side of the street,
I didn't burn in a long day's sun;
I sat on a porch and read and waited
for an echo of pain from the cotton fields.

Later I thought I had a right to the blues,
could make the passion count;
I thought I had a right to the blues,
to the hidden tears that Minnie shed.

She held me in her arms without a tear,
not when she held me in her arms
and sang quietly of another time,
and held me with comfort deep in her voice.

I thought that gave me a right to sing;
I thought I had shared her pain,
an echo of an older pain;
and now she's gone and free of pain,

I'm left to wonder if I'll ever sing,
if I can echo a bit of her pain;
but now I know I've no right to the pain,
no right to the songs she sang.

I never was able to tell her
she pulled me through childish pain
while quietly she slipped away
into an echo of remembered pain.

And when, years later, we met and hugged,
she held herself back from the pain
we'd shared; she held herself back
and left me alone to sing the blues.

And now I wish to sing what she knew,
I wish that I could sing the pain;
but I was from another side of the street
and tried in the rain to sing the blues.

I thought I could learn to sing the blues,
could make the passion count;
I thought I had a right to the blues
because they're still a part of me.

But I've no right to the blues she knew,
never could know the passion she felt,
though I wanted to sing the blues,
wanted to make her passion count.

I'm left with a song to murmur softly,
left with a pain that still cuts deep,
left with words to whisper aloud
how I wish that I could sing the blues.

HANGING TREE

They hung him in a tree, that's what the man said;
he hung there 'til he was dead.
That's what the man said.

They hung him in a tree 'cause he sassed the sheriff
and may have laughed a little
for that's the way he was.

He may have laughed 'til he was dead.
They hung him in a pine tree.
That's what the man said.

They hung him in a tree 'cause he sassed the sheriff;
they hung him there until he was stiff.
It's what the man said.

He hung there and laughed until he was dead.
That wasn't so long ago
is what the man said.

They hung him in a pine tree until he died;
and he laughed and laughed until he cried.
That's what the man said.

GROWING UP WITH THE BLUES

I grew up in the black arms of those who sang,
the black arms that held me close and sang
with a sound of voices pullin' me into growin' up.

    Shall I try again to sing the blues,
    even when you know I can't sing the blues?

I grew up lovin' Minnie who cared for me,
a large mama who cared for me and held me in her arms
a long time ago, before I realized I was growin' up.

    Shall I try again to write the blues,
    shall I try again to sing the blues?

The world was black and I loved it that way
and didn't know I was just a poor stray
white boy who didn't know he was growin' up.

    Shall I try again in age to sing the blues,
    though I write poems I call the blues?

The world is black from the fires we light;
the blues are in the air we breathe;
and it's been that way since we started growing up.

    Shall I try again and chant the blues,
    shall I try again to whisper the blues?

FAILURE OF THE BLUES

I try to sing the blues, they turn to poems;
I want those loved long ago to reappear
in words I hear during a restless night.

I scrawl across a scrap of paper a holler
gathered by a kid from all those workers
in tobacco fields and from Minnie as she cooked.

I never sweat enough to make it real;
it turns to an egoistic melody
that tries to use a syntax that's learned.

I can't match the power of the holler,
for Minnie bathed me when I hurt, and sang
until I slept and dreamed of mules that danced.

I find no voices that will echo mine
with harsh realities of an open field;
my voice is rattling in an empty room.

WORDS DON'T GET THROUGH

It's heart breaking when words don't get through,
even though in all these words there's nothing new.

They don't get through, they fall into an empty ditch,
and get flushed in the next rain,
a rich supplement for compost that stinks.

It happens often that the words don't get through,
even if they lack anything that's new.

They don't get through, they hang on the edge of space,
hanging out there where the stars all race
to find their way through dark puddles of ink.

How often have words ever got through?
How often have they ever carried anything new?

They don't get through, they linger on a page
get shuffled to the bottom like spent rage,
and over the years they crumble and fade.

It's heart breaking when these words fall through
and leave me with nothing to send on to you.

COTTON FIELD BLUES

I.

It was part of waking, to hear their voices singing
among groves below my grandmother's house,
with words I could not understand, a cry
of words, a cry to anticipate the day.

They climbed the hill, and I climbed from bed
and quietly ran to the porch to watch them pass,
their mules in polished leather, the sun still cool
over pecan trees, their voices deep.

A heavy voice rumbled about heavy clay,
not made, he sang, for play, as others made
a sound like drums and bells and pipes, the words
a blur of rhythms to lift with hope.

Melodious and sad, but full of strength,
they followed muddy paths and dropped the song
in ditches behind mules, unloaded knives
and hoes and hunkered to a sweaty task.

It was still too early for grits and eggs,
and so, before returning to my bed,
I went to greet grandfather, sitting under
a peach tree in the garden, reading his bible.

2.

The day would pass in a casual way, with walks
to town, a lunch and naps, perhaps a story
from Clara Mae, a song at the old piano,
and regular trips to the outhouse in the garden.

"We'll sing," our Granny said, and lifted her voice
in an imitation of the songs I'd heard
as they had climbed the hill. It wasn't the same;
it lacked the flame, the need. It was amusing.

But as sun went down, I heard voices,
much slower now, in a cracked sound of pain
as they left cotton fields and came down the hill,
just there, beyond a swing on the old front porch.

The mules were dragging and piled with bags
of cotton, the wagon creaked and swayed; as old men
chanted, a woman's voice rose high and sharp,
and children cried, but not a dog would bark.

"The day's done gone," a voice sang deep;
"The night's come on," another voice broke in.
The voices of the women trailed after,
"It ain't much further we got to go."

3.

A voice from the house called us to supper, ignored
the mules and men who slowly passed and children
huddled behind a group of women who sang
their chant of pain that was tired of the day.

Later, as I lay in bed and listened
to a night of restless wind in trees,
a cry still lingered like a memory
of ghosts in blue smoke: "Oh my, oh my….

"This cry's the song you hear when you hear the voice
that cries the notes that linger in your heart
that aches like the muscles in your back. Oh my.
Oh my…." It was the song I heard as I slept.

Can you hear it echo in the night
and bet against the failure of memory?
I woke that night with my own sweat of terror,
squatted on the slop jar and slept again.

That was years ago, and sometimes I wake
and whisper to myself, "The day's done gone;
the dark's fallin' here for good. Oh my…;"
and then I hear the voices calling at dawn.

ALL MY SONS

"You is my son," she said, "and your daddy
and his daddy too; you is all my sons."

The walls of the shack were papered with comics
and bright ads, relieved in places by a patterned
white and black of classified sheets.

And she said, "You is my son, and your daddy
and his daddy too; you is all my sons."

The bed was covered with a pad of straw
that rustled when she shook with winter chills,
though it was hot and my shirt stuck to my back.

"My name is the same as yours," she said;
"you is my son; you is all my sons."

I thought I'd be thrilled to see a woman
pass a hundred years, but behind my father,
I could only cry, and my shirt stuck to my back.

"My daddy told me that we was free," she said;
" 'Kitty, we is free,' he said. 'We is free,' is what he said."

I itched as a swarm of flies circled her eyes,
her glittering eyes, and settled on my neck, crawled
in my hair as I held my hands in a sweaty fist.

"You is my son," she said, "and your daddy is my son;
and his daddy too; you is all my sons."

For more than a hundred years she lived right here,
a hundred years in a one-room shack;
only the comics were new, only the paper on the wall.

And though her voice faded, I can hear her say,
still hear her say, "You is my son and your daddy too."

GETTING IT RIGHT

We never seem to get it right —
        there're some things we never get right.
We push up and down the hills —
        more slowly as years accumulate,
more slowly wondering why not even love
        forgives us the horror of what's been done,
of what we're doing still — a thousand here
        ten thousand there, or even one or two.

The one who died because he was black,
        the one who hung until he was dead....
"I loved him," I cry. "It wasn't I."
        I cry and try to climb another hill.
But it was done. As long as any one can do it
        to another, I'll carry the pain.
We have to carry the pain,
        otherwise we'd never get it right.

We can learn to love in spite of it all —
        in spite of what others may do,
in spite of what we ourselves could do
        if we'd not been taught to love
by Minnie who held us in her arms to teach us love
        and Kitty who folded us into one family;
and yet we seem unable to get it right —
        some things we just never seem to get right.

SOON GONE

She denies that she's a Lilith.
"I don't even know who she is," she says;
"never even heard her name until
you started droppin' these crazy poems."

"I work everyday," she says. "Every day.
And I got another grandchild comin' soon."
She groans and stretches for her sweater
before she plops a mug and a smile.

She starts to turn away, but pauses
and turns back. "There'll come a time
we won't be here any more;
we'll not be there, anywhere, just dust."

She pauses. "But as long as I'm here I'm gonna
enjoy, gonna hold my head high and laugh."
She doesn't even try to catch my eye;
she's looking out the window, out back,

perhaps at her car, a rusty old car covered
with bumper stickers, the joke of the cooks
in the kitchen: "Not all who wander are lost,"
a sticker says, in a little something from Tolkein;

"Lez Danze," another says, though scratched
with artificial laughter that waits for the end
of her shift and a fast trip home. She soon returns
without a smile, but with a fresh mug.

"Chances are," she says as she pauses...,
"chances are we'll soon be gone.
It's what the song says that the singer sang
last night — we'll soon be gone."

GREETINGS FOR A NEW YEAR

Where is she? I ask, unexpectedly,
in the middle of a lunch of nothing special,
while we read diatribes that we cheer on
by Maureen Dowd. She's usually in Boston,
she says, not asking which she I might mean.
But for this long? I say, not as a question,
just a passing comment as her image passes
through a flickering file of memories.
She's like a self-portrait by that young Russian,
I say. Perhaps her grandfather was Russian,
she says. But it's been so long, I say.
She's fine, she says; she has to get away.
What if you worked there? I'd quit, I say.
Maybe..., she says. No, no, no, I say: she can't.

Quit worrying, she says. I don't, I say;
I just miss her, that's all. So do I, she says,
flickering through pages for something
that might cheer us on for the new year.
Well, this comic won't do it, I say,
throwing down the local rag that's a bore.
Well then, she says, we'll just think of her:
that's enough to cheer up an old year
and get us prepared for a better one.
Cheers, I say; too bad it's just lunch time
and we won't open wine until later.
That's when we'll raise our glasses in a toast
to her, she says; she'll know: she'll taste it;
she'll pull it out of air in spite of the news.

NO CALL

I was afraid you'd never call.
We wander half-way through a winter storm
and stop to catch our breath
and leave a curt message with your service.
But still no word.

I wonder if you're still around
or if you finally had to close down.
We hear you got warned off
and probably responded with a shrug.
It's what you'd do.

But why no call or just a note?
The storm lets up, we wander on our way;
but not without concern
for the mad girl who used to say she knew
that we would call.

You're not the only one who's gone;
so many have slipped away this winter,
it might as well be you.
We'll try again if we ever get home.
Maybe we'll hear.

TO SING AGAIN

We settle at table, order salads,
open books, ready now to exchange quotations,
when a voice drifts, with a sigh, from behind me:
"…All I want to do is sit on the piano
and sing again…." Whatever else she says
is lost in the clatter of the room or my head.
My book falls shut and my companion almost laughs.
She knows I have a weakness for sad club singers,
the ones who prowled cafés in Paris
when I was young enough to think dreams might prevail.
I wait to hear if the voice has an accent.

I want to turn, but hesitate, afraid
it will be another face from the neighborhood
like all the others, aging and well groomed, smiling
at appropriate moments, the way we all do.
"I'm not at all sure which one she is," my friend says;
"perhaps the older one facing us, full of tears."
They are always full of tears, I think, and passion
for what has happened to their world. I remember
standing within the gates of a cemetery
trying to hear a famous singer as she moved
among crowded tables I could not afford.

Making an excuse, I go to look at pastries,
bitter chocolate wrapped in dough provides a slight
distraction from three women in conversation,
one of whom might be a nostalgic singer.
When she looks up and smiles, I almost stumble:
I would like to think, would like to say, it is she
who sat on a piano in a crowded room
and whispered sad songs that, after fifty years,
still linger in the rhythms of memory.
I respond with a smile and wonder if she
would laugh and offer to sing among the pastries.

ON THE TELEPHONE

She speaks as sun breaks free, but the telephone
crackles so sharply I can't hear a word;
the wind rattles against the window
where I stand watching birds dart for shelter
through trees that fold upon themselves
or sweep the sky as, once again, sun fades.

She speaks, wondering why I've not replied,
why I haven't told her; but what, I think I say,
is there to say, wondering if a dragon
that slips through high circles above the fields
knows what's happening down here
at the window or among buffeted trees.

She speaks again, in a voice of agitation,
as clouds for a moment pull themselves apart
and leave a strip of blue hanging like a banner,
ragged and defiant, as if clouds are Himalayan,
distant and cold where banners are hung
as reminders that life continues in spite of all.

She speaks louder, perhaps a little harshly;
she wants reassurance, I think it is;
but clouds have closed in once again, darker;
and the dragon cries one last time and slips
to a distant hill, to his own dark assurance;
and, with reluctance, I sever the connection.

MAGDALENE

"You don't understand," she said, looking me
directly in the eye. "It isn't she. It's I.
They took her name and labeled me a whore.
They lied as they usually do on Sunday mornings
or Saturday dinners when families gather close."

She spat over the rail into the canal, a drop
that swirled and, for a moment, attracted local gulls.
A waiter hesitated and turned away. I watched
the gulls rise and slip downwind for other remains
as I still wondered what she might be all about.

"Just call me Maggie," she said. We'd seen each other
several times when I slipped in for prosecco at noon."
But who was the other one, I kept asking myself;
the one who always flew away as darkness fell,
who flew and lifted herself high among the towers.

And that's when bells rang, when she was there
as bells rang with incontinence, as if with a voice
a dragon had carried across interminable time.
"I'm confused," I said, clearing my throat, trying
to decide just who was who in this dyadal riddle.

"There seem to be two of you," I said, "like twins...,"
which brought her to laughter — at least a laugh
of exasperation. "She's older," she said. "Much older.
But she escaped. They took her name and she escaped
and left me to watch my sisters fade away."

"Now I must go," she said. "I've got to see
another sister in the mountains; but I'll be back.
Listen for the owls and that will let you know
I'm on my way. At least one of us will come,
will see you here if not another place or time."

OLD ACTRESS

1.

She moves into old age as she moves across the stage,
a lingering glance at the audience, a pause, a smile.
It does not matter that it is a play of tragic dimensions,
that she will leave the stage to die, that she has lost
so much as years have passed and wars come and go;
it's still a role that she can play. She knows just when
to turn her back and slowly lift her shoulders and sigh
and bring a tear to half the audience, even if some laugh
and whisper, "Come on, my dear, we've seen enough
of that; fifty years ago you found that gesture worked,
whether we were meant to laugh or cry or even yawn."
And still we come to see her move through space,
move from dark to light, until the lights go out
and she's left a shadow waiting for a curtain call.

2.

When I was twenty-two I saw her dance across a stage,
moving with the flexibility of a dragon in a language
I did not know and did not need to know: She entered
and carried each phrase across the foot lights to us,
each of us, in a dark auditorium; she moved mysteriously
as each of the other actors disappeared, and only she,
only this graceful, frightening creature was there, alone,
at the center of a small stage, demanding our attention,
reaching for us, even if there were only a few of us
in a small basement theatre with a small stage
that we could reach and touch as she turned her back
and shrugged, and a chill moved down my back
and, as lanterns faded and we were left in the dark,
I was convinced I'd seen something powerful and unique.

3.

She'll move again across the stage when I am gone;
some kid who plays with words will think he's seen it all
now that he's seen this new young star, this fierce face,
this hint of something more, almost like a dragon
in a new constellation that's just beginning to show,
after a few million years, a force that seems so new
this kid will think he's found it all for the first time,
or so he will by the time he's old, by the time they're gone
again through the sweeping heart of time, their time,
much like what I had thought was the heart of my time.
Again, she'll turn her back and shrug and he will feel
the thrill of having seen something new; until, that is,
he finds the ancient books, the tales, and knows that she
lingers through time as a power that was meant to be.

TOSHIKO'S BELL MOVES IN

When Harry and Wendy arrive mid-day and I see this giant
      awkwardly wrapped bell teetering on their truck, I am
      apprehensive, for we've had a long-time rule here
      that no piece of art should be larger than a human being —
      after all, the only thing potentially as important, if shorter
      lived, than a work of art, is a human.

But then I am utterly distracted and fascinated by the way Wendy
      and Harry work and relax over lunch while my guys
      prepare the spot, especially when, later, the bell is lifted,
      still wrapped, and begins its swinging journey, very much
      like a Lilith, like a flying dragon, from truck to designated
      spot some 30' away.

Suddenly, the wraps are off and Wendy and Harry step back,
      my guys go silent, and there she is, waiting, as if
      she has always been there, waiting there, as if she
      has been conceived just for this spot and no other; so it is
      time, I know, to use the mallet, a perfectly moldy old mallet
      that I have been armed with while waiting.

I approach her and touch her flesh with affectionate gentleness:
      a sound swells and rises through the front courtyard, rises
      through linden and oak trees, rises higher than the house,
      wondering where Toshiko is, where her hands are — and so
      I strike harder and the sounds laugh and so does everyone,
      as the bell tones a feel of home, for it is at home.

I'm still amazed, humbled, exalted, mystified, delighted,
      and full of deep pleasure as everyone sticks a head
      into the cavity of the bell and she vibrates and her voice
      becomes a part of each of us, something else within us;
      and we climb to windows and look to see her, most beautiful,
      in a world that is art when seen from the music room.

Among greenery (and I'm sure snow), she settles in,
        looking up when Andrea comes in to play her flute
        right in that window, not five feet away; where, when I come
        and head to the large black piano, I pause and wonder
        whether she would prefer Bach or Chopin for the afternoon
        and swear she echoes Schumann played this morning.

We are thrilled to have her, not "in our collection", for no one
        can possess Toshiko's Bell, but living with us here
        where gardens flourish, where fruits ripen and summer roses
        enflame the berm, and the retrievals of life fill the land
        with enriching compost and a high nest for restless,
        persistent owls of Lilith waiting for an evening flight.

In the night I wake and hear the bell surround the house
        with its presence, hear its passionate response to reminders
        that winds carry, hear its reminders of a great artist,
        a great woman who has led us through haunting possibilities
        that too often disappear and leave us lying awake wondering
        when her vibrancies will come again.

LILITH AS A MUSICIAN

Could she have been a musician,
could she have composed a piano sonata?
Or would her flame have burnt the chord,
consumed the keys, melted ivory?

Could she have been a mezzo,
a burr in the voice to burn the heart?

That's more like it.
                      I heard that voice
and had to fight to regain breath,
a calm attenuation of my lungs.
It was a while before I could even say
a word to my companion
as we walked the park
looking at the moon and wondering
if that wasn't a dragon cutting the glare.

A friend, a conductor, used to swear
it was impossible to hold her to the page,
that no tenor would share his voice
to die or love or rise in splendor
as curtains fall and the audience
gasps in wonder at what is going on.

They are often called divas;
but being a diva is just a role
like any other.
                  She doesn't play a role;
she lives with the ferocity of night
when storms come rumbling in from the sea.

That's what the audience wants to see and hear,
if only from the comfort of heated seats;
that's what, I must admit, I look for
when I spend an hour at the piano
alone, except for passion that can
be found in a bit of Beethoven.

Even now, in age, fingers stumble
over the idea of Lilith,
across the heated breath that lingers
in fluctuations of chords that rise
and fall and fade away.
                          I sit back
and take a deeper breath and try
to calm that breath, to pull back
from where, I suddenly realize,
I could have gone if I had tried,
if there was still that moment of youth,
that energy that carried a bit of her.

But could she have done it?
Or is she the it itself, the music
without the aging hands, the voice
that reaches with all the power
the rest of us have lost.

It's she I listen for. It's she I hear,
the music itself that pulls
across the afternoon and clears the sky
for the moon, the owls,
the melodious stirring of the night.

HER WORDS FALL

A few words, just words, a few
              to float down this page,
through the space of this page

as we look into a white summer sky
              and see these words,
and see her hovering right there,

see her circling with her dragon,
              right there
on a bright page of an afternoon.

And if we listen with affectionate attention,
              really listen,
we hear the harsh laughter of her dragon,

and a falling, sharp gail of laughter
              that has to be her, an old friend,
an occasional friend who can't resist

another scattering of words
              down across the space of this page,
to fill the bright emptiness that's no longer empty.

See, just a few words
              float down this page,
not knowing where they will cease,

somewhere here, right here, now,
              approaching the bottom of the page
as her laughter grows full and immediate.

LOVE'S DANCE

1.

She rears like Lilith, pulls back and laughs;
he stutters and crushes his hearing aid.
She stretches to feel her image crack
with aging limps; he longs for a goddess
who'll yawn all morning under a red umbrella
and sleep with dreams of another day
while he waits beneath a billowing tent.

If either sees me typing these words
in a flow and a pause to delete a phrase
or add a beat that'll stretch the time
to hear me whisper to the screen "Not that;
it's something else," they hoot with laughter
and know I'll turn the tale again
to Venus and a little guy she loved.

It's always someone Ares shuffled,
Achilles or Lilith or Aphrodite.
So they are stuck with images that lay
a tune across the page, as he plays
for girls to dance, and, in the quiet,
calls them dragons and laughs or cries
at silence others will stretch to find.

2.

There's always something else, a wash
of yellow, another shade of gray,
a rhythmic move, as she crosses the years
to watch Lilith ride the day
in search of revenge. It's closer now;
it's that or total fadeaway —
with no other hearing aid to smash.

We pay attention when we should sleep
as fires fade over there or rage;
for stumbling on steps is another part
of getting through a day with songs
the sirens sing, with the beauty of Charybdis.
We know that grumbles stir an image,
that being tied to the mast saved Odysseus.

So let her laugh or snort indignation,
we listen for echoes from a distant cave
as he wraps himself in dreams; and I slam
a door and pour words and hope
there'll be a little bronze to place
beside my chair as I read the stories
and wonder if anyone is left to hear.

3.

Do I speak of myself or others I've known?
I never know: Winds bring whispers
of what it's all about as I wander
the night and listen for dragons and hear
deep songs and wonder if they will linger
in words I whisper to myself, words
that are nothing I hear beyond the owls.

It was twenty years before he returned
for a great to-do, and the studio grew calm.
But who can settle for a quiet old age?
So he left again and followed the sun
for tales told in beautiful ways.
I like to think that somewhere at dusk
he joins our Lilith on a noisy beach.

The sun sets and rises beyond the horizon
as he pushes paint, ignores the ranting,
dreams music that he carries into age;
and she watches for sailors tied to a mast
and belches anger at betrayals of her race;
through a day of heat and sealed windows,
I try to find a rhythm for their dance.

4.

She's always there, our Lilith; she sings
through densities of time, alone or with
that little fellow who's stuck around.
They give me beats I've got to keep,
movement I could never find when I
was young and tried to give a thrill
to blondes who had no hint of Lilith.

It's not the figure at the bottom of the stair
that brings some visitors to panic;
she's always there, reminder of power
that tears her skin away. It's the other
whose voice is hidden in trees at night,
who hoots like an owl and blocks the moon,
the one who always reminds me of you.

Whoever 'you' may be, I hope
you know, when we are dust in drifts
beneath the door that settles on roses,
we'll keep the deadness on the other side,
as she lunges at the world to make us duck.
We need to open doors for the dance
to echo across hills and come to rest.

I have hidden within hollow trees so that I might watch and listen for the approach of Lilith; and there she would be, behind the counter, with a deep southern accent — and I'd suddenly be 70 years back in Georgia encountering field-holler blues as workers and mules climb past grandmother's house to cotton fields.

Every poem is an encounter and my favorite embody Lilith; in fact, the rebelliousness and pang of a poem itself is Lilithian.

The musician, physician, photographer with whom I share my life may or may not be a Lilith, but she brought me a Tara, the Lilithian mother of wrathful Buddha, from the Himalayas and pokes and prods that power with her camera.

BOOKS OF POEMS BY HOLLIS

EARLY ENCOUNTERS

LETTERS AND VOICES FROM THE STEPPES

MIDLIFE ENCOUNTERS

SKETCHES FOR A MAYAN ODYSSEY

SCENES FROM AN OLD ALBUM

SONATA SONNETS

LAS ESPINAS

LETTER POEMS

VENETIAN VARIATIONS

DARK ENCOUNTER IN MID AIR

POEM-CHANTING TOWER

LILITH AND THE BLUES

BOOKS OF PHOTOGRAPHS BY BALDECK

THE HEART OF HAITI

TALISMANIC

VENICE A PERSONAL VIEW

TOUCHING THE MEKONG

CLOSELY OBSERVED

PRESENCE PASSING

HIMALAYA: LAND OF THE SNOW LION

Design and production of this book were managed by
Veronica Miller & Associates, Haverford, Pennsylvania.
Production supervision was provided by Peter Philbin.
The book was printed by Brilliant Graphics, Exton, Pennsylvania
and was bound by Hoster Book Bindery, Ivyland, Pennsylvania.